Cheap
Psychological
Tricks
for Lovers

Cheap Psychological Tricks for Lovers

55 Savvy Strategies for the Romantically Challenged

Perry W. Buffington, Ph.D.

Illustrated by
Jen Singh

PEACHTREE
ATLANTA

Published by
PEACHTREE PUBLISHERS LTD.
494 Armour Circle NE
Atlanta, Georgia 30324

www.peachtree-online.com

Book and cover design by Loraine M. Balcsik
Book composition by Melanie M. McMahon

Manufactured in the United States of America

10 9 8 7 6 5 4 3 2 1
First Edition

Library of Congress Cataloging-in-Publication Data

Buffington, Perry W.
   Cheap psychological tricks for lovers : 55 savvy strategies for the romantically challenged / Perry W. Buffington ; illustrated by Jen Singh.-- 1st ed.
      p. cm.
Includes bibliographical references.
   ISBN 1-56145-218-1
   1. Man-woman relationships. 2. Mate selection 3. Men--Psychology. 4. Women--Psychology. 5. Dating (Social customs) I. Title.
   HQ801 .B875 2000
   646. 7'7--dc21

                        00-010638

Table of Contents

Part III Pairing:
Getting It on Together

Part IV Affairing and Repairing:
Navigating the Rocky Road of Romance

Part V Sharing

Spending the Rest of Your Life Together

Introduction

Here's one of life's little realities. Men may be from that warring planet Mars, and women may have originated on that beautiful planet Venus, but all of us are stuck on Earth. And even though romantic love may be dying on the evolutionary vine, you still have more than enough time to snare and to care for that life mate, especially if you have the right technique, know what you're doing, don't mind using a few cheap psychological tricks designed for the relationship challenged—and have $9.95 to pay for this book.

Within these covers, you'll find real research, fun-to-read examples, and absolutely no psychobabble. You'll see new findings from recent decades, old ideas from the early 1900s and late 1800s made new again, and even a little Greek philosophy. At the end of every trick you'll find one or more reference citations showing you where to learn more about the science behind the trick.

Don't get caught up in the word "trick." Think of these "tricks" as honest, responsible applications that may improve the odds that your love will last a lifetime.

REFERENCE

Gray, J. *Men are from Mars, Women are from Venus: A Practical Guide for Improving Communication and Getting What You Want in Your Relationships.* New York: Harper Collins, 1992.

PART I

Snaring

Finding That Perfect Mate!

Venus favors the bold.
—Ovid

Near Heart, Dear Heart

If you want to purchase a car, you go to a car lot. If you want to be an actor or actress, you go to auditions. If you want to buy a horse, you visit a stable. Get the idea? If you want a mate, you've got to go where the prospects are, and that's where the laws of propinquity come in to play.

Propinquity is a fancy word for "nearness." The law of propinquity states that we are more attracted to those people we see on a regular basis. In other words, if you see people regularly in familiar surroundings, it's not unusual to strike up a conversation with them, make friends, and perhaps even establish a relationship. This law explains why so many single people who live in apartment complexes get married to someone who lives in the same complex.

So, if you want to find a mate, you must go where potential mates congregate, such as church, synagogue, service club meetings, charity fund-raisers, and or some other locale that fits your interests. But there's a psychological twist to the tryst. Aim for the middle!

Think back to high school. You'll probably recall that the most popular students sat together in the middle of the room, while everyone else had to sit and watch from the fringes. The same phenomenon occurs in apartment complexes. Often the most popular people are those who have the middle apartment where the world seems to revolve around them. Taking the middle seat in church will increase the number of people who notice you. This also explains why the corner office, in the middle of the action, is so coveted.

Humans are conditioned to look to the middle first. Studies have shown that most people will choose the middle stall when they enter a public bathroom. Trying to select a box of cereal? Chances are you'll pick a box out of the middle, even if you have a wide variety from which to choose. Why? The middle feels safer, more comfortable.

To find a mate, put the two tricks together. Use the laws of propinquity to find a place where potential partners congregate. Don't expect to find someone the first meeting—unless you're lucky. Propinquity works best over time because it breeds safety through familiarity. Now to be the belle—or beau—of the ball, place yourself squarely in the middle of the room. That way the party will revolve around you. Isn't that the way the world should be?

One disclaimer: Research shows that laws of propinquity do not work for irritating people. If this trick doesn't work for you, don't blame this book.

What's the cheap psychological trick? Use the law of propinquity and go to the places where you're most likely to find potential mates. Once you get there, head to the center of the crowd. You should be in the right place to make a love connection.

REFERENCES

"Bathroom Behavior." *Psychology Today* 30 February (1997): 20.

Festinger, L., S. Schachter, and K. Back. *Social Pressures in Informal Groups. A Study of Human Factors in Housing.* New York: Harper Bros, 1950.

Cheap Trick No. 2

Practically Perfect
Personal Ad

Thousands of personal ads are placed and read each day in newspapers around the world. Purchase a paper and you can find lonely hearts, just like you, looking for love. When you use the personal ads, the list of possible love connections is right there in front of you. It's an easy, unending source of possibilities. Who knows? The love of your life could be right there just waiting for you to call.

Personal ads are a veritable cornucopia of wish lists written by everyday folk. Some ads are effective, and others are no better than the most pathetic pickup line you've heard in a bar. Want to write an ad that will get the most response? Consider your approach carefully.

Personal ads typically fall into one of three categories: direct, hard-to-get, and humorous. As a general rule, nix the wit; even hard-to-get will get you further than funny. But your best bet is to be direct.

Bear in mind that it's not what *you* want that matters, it's what the reader wants. To get a favorable response, write your personal ad from the reader's perspective.

Women generally respond to personal ads offering security and resources. Men base their choices on physical attractiveness. If you decide to place a personal ad, keep these observations in mind. Men, play up your ability to offer future security in your ads. Women, emphasize your good looks.

One little psychological curiosity. There's something about using the word "redhead" that may give you a competitive edge. The reason behind this phenomenon is unknown. It may be a throwback to the time when prostitutes were required to dye their hair red. Maybe we're just conditioned to think that red is the color of passion. But no matter the reason, if you're a redhead—real or bottled—use it in your ad. You'll get more responses.

What's the cheap psychological trick? Cut to the chase and give the reader what they want. And if you're not a redhead, you might consider a visit with Miss Clairol in order to get a better response.

REFERENCES

Buss, D. M. "The Evolution of Desire: The Strategies of Human Mating," *American Scientist* 82 (1994): 238–249.

Cunningham, M.R. "Reactions to Heterosexual Opening Gambits: Female Selectivity and Male Responsiveness," *Personality & Social Psychology Bulletin* 15 (1989): 27–41.

Rajecki, D. W., S.B. Bledsoe, and J.L. Rasmussen. "Successful Personal Ads: Gender differences and similarities in offers, stipulations and outcomes." *Basic and Applied Social Psychology* 12 (1991): 457–469.

Increase Your Options

If you're looking for love at the bar, forget those tired old pickup lines. The odds of them working are just not on your side. There's another approach to picking up dates at bars and it's practically guaranteed. It's all in the timing—time of night, that is.

Researchers asked the patrons of several bars to rate potential dates on a scale of one to ten. The people judged most attractive were rated ten; the least attractive were rated one. As the evening progressed, the patrons were more and more likely to describe as attractive those they'd previously found less attractive.

The results were essentially the same for both genders. Both sexes became equally jaded as the night wore on. The scores of both men and women once rated as unattractive climbed higher and higher toward acceptable as closing time approached.

What's the cheap psychological trick? If you want to feel popular at your local pub, stay late—or show up just before closing time. Even if you're not generally considered attractive, you'll have the pick of the litter. Of course, you need to keep in mind the kind of litter from which you'll be picking.

REFERENCES

Knight, B. "Don't the Girls Get Prettier at Closing Time." Singletree Music (BMI), Division of Merit Music Corporation, 1975.

Nida, S.A., and J. Koon. "They Get Better Looking at Closing Time around Here, too." *Psychological Reports* 52 (1983): 657–658.

Pennebaker, J.W., M.A. Dyer, R.S. Caulkins, D.L. Litowitz, P.L. Ackerman, D. G. Anderson, and K.M. McGraw. "Don't the Girls Get Prettier at Closing Time: A Country and Western Application to Psychology." *Personality & Social Psychology Bulletin* 5 (1979): 122–125.

Steinberg, R.J. "Love as a Story." *Journal of Social and Personal Relationships* 12 (1995): 541–546.

Cheap Trick No. 4

A Trick Question

Almost all men—and some women—have fantasized about approaching someone they find attractive and saying, "Let's have sex." Finally, research offers insight into how this sexual fantasy might play out in real life.

Assume you see someone for the first time. What would happen if you opened with this line: "I've been noticing you. I find you very attractive. Would you go to bed with me tonight?" You're in for a surprise answer.

Real scientists tried this approach on a variety of people. Here are the results: Not one woman agreed to go to bed with a stranger who uttered only these three sentences. Men, however, started removing their clothes on the spot. According to the researchers, the men's attitude was "Why wait until tonight?" Two out of three men, said, "Yeah, baby!" Those men who didn't accept this invitation felt compelled to explain why they couldn't: "I'm seeing someone." "I'm gay." "I've got an appointment tonight. How about tomorrow night?"

When the researchers changed the approach—"I've been noticing you. I find you very attractive. Will you go on a date with me?"—there was a 50-50 chance that both men and women would say yes.

What's the cheap psychological trick? It can't hurt to ask for what you want, but if you're a man and you want sex from a strange woman, you're probably out of luck. Better ask her for a date first.

If you're a woman and you only want sex, chances are good that the stranger will be happy to oblige. But if you'd rather ask for a date first (which we'd recommend), your odds are pretty favorable, too.

REFERENCES

Baumeister, R. F., and M.R. Leary. "The Need to Belong: Desire for Interpersonal Attachments as a Fundamental Human Motivation." *Psychological Bulletin* 117 (1995): 497–529.

Clark, R .D., and E. Hatfield. "Gender Differences in Receptivity to Sexual Offers." *Journal of Psychology and Human Sexuality* 2 (1989): 39–55.

Cheap Dates

There are some cheap men out there, and you can spot them before it's too late. During the courtship phase, money is no object to this cheap lover. This type of potential partner will spend, spend, spend in order to impress a would-be mate and invest whatever it takes to snare the love of a lifetime. But after this free-spending mate has convinced you to make a commitment, you may wake up to find that you're involved with the cheapest, stingiest, most penny-pinching person in the world. Too bad you didn't know to listen for a certain telltale sign.

Jingling pocket change is a statement of personality and serves a purpose. This kind of behavior is technically referred to as a "Type B" attachment—a pattern in which people in strange situations or under stress use some person, place, or thing as a base of security and as a means to regain the source of that security. The behavior—jingling his pocket change—began as a security blanket, as a way of proving that he had money, and now it has become a habit. Just as a young child needs his favorite stuffed animal, the adult now needs to hear the sound of change jingling to reduce anxiety, to hold the fear of poverty at bay, and to provide comfort.

What's the cheap psychological trick? Listen for the jingling of change in your partner's pocket. It may be a signal that this person is cheap, and you'll have to deal with this as long as your relationship lasts.

REFERENCE

Main, M., and J. Solomon. "Procedure for Identifying Infants as Disorganized/Disoriented during the Ainsworth Strange Situation." In M.T. Greenberg, D. Cicchetti, and E.M. Cummings (Eds.), *Attachment in the Preschool Years: Theory, Research, and Intervention.* Chicago: University of Chicago Press, 1990.

SWAK–Sealed With a Kiss!

There's more to the humble kiss than mouth meeting mouth. Romans so loved the kiss that their Latin language is alive with variations on a kissable theme. For instance, an *osculum* is a kiss on the face or cheeks. Take it one step further, and it becomes a *basium*, or an affectionate kiss. Next, there's the no-holds-barred kiss, the *suavium*, for lovers only.

Unfortunately today the kiss is often overlooked. Many couples forget to kiss and most sex researchers ignore the power of the kiss. Kissing was not even addressed in the landmark University of Chicago Sex in America survey in 1994.

When it comes to kissing in our era, the following observational statistics (rounded up or down) apply to both genders:

☀ 90% like kissing

☀ 90% enjoy kissing in their car

☼ 90% enjoy being kissed on the ear

☼ 80% enjoy a gentle bite when kissed

☼ 50% say that kissing is more intimate than sex

☼ 40% find kissing essential after a fight

☼ 40% would kiss more if they had the time

☼ 25% enjoy necking in the movies

The kiss has two elements, sensation and motor, and burns about six to twelve calories per pucker. The sensory stimulation of a kiss is controlled by the fifth cranial nerve, whose upper and lower divisions control both the upper and lower lip, respectively. Thank the seventh cranial nerve—the facial nerve—for the pucker. Putting this physiology together, you come up with this pleasant chain of events. You feel with the fifth nerve, then pucker up with the seventh, which causes you to feel more, which further stimulates the fifth nerve, which causes the seventh nerve to generate a greater pucker. This wonderful cycle continues for about one minute,

KISS ME

the time of the average kiss. The stimulation of both nerves causes the glands in the mouth and the lips to secrete saliva, and that's important.

Some researchers believe that kissing is actually the beginning of a chemical bond that can unite people for a lifetime. Apparently it's the ingestion of each other's sebum (the semiliquid, greasy secretion of the sebaceous glands) that does the trick. Chemicals found in humble saliva are thought to be among those that attract one human to another. Sebum excretion levels are highest during early adulthood—the period when bonding is most important. In other words, when the desire for courtship is strong, sebum is abundant. Some studies have shown that you will kiss at least seventy-nine people before you find your ideal mate.

What's the cheap psychological trick? Kiss a lot. Once you find the perfect sebum, you've found your mate for life.

REFERENCE

Bakos, S. *Sexational Secrets: Erotic Advice Your Mother Never Gave You.* New York: St. Martin's Mass Market Paper Press, 1998.

Sweet and Sour Sex

It's absolutely impossible to visit a fashionable department store in an upscale mall without being accosted by perfume spritzers. They're on every aisle extolling the specific virtues of the fragrance du jour. Perfume is big business, and consumers shell out big bucks just to smell attractive to the opposite gender. So, before you buy a $100 ounce of "Tonight's the Night," maybe you ought to check out these cheap psychological fragrances.

First, some odors do indeed enhance romance, but not the ones you would expect. And, yes, they are different for men and women.

According to some studies, women are aroused by the smell of cucumber and sweet licorice. Researchers also noted that cherry flavor inhibits female sexual desire. Most men's fragrances also inhibited sexual desire. The hoped-for turn-on was a turnoff—no matter what the slick advertising implied.

Further proof that the fastest way to a man's heart is through the stomach: researchers found that men were turned on by—you'll never guess—pumpkin. Men also really responded to another fragrance, one that your grandmother and her mother before her probably wore. Men responded sexually to the smell of lavender. As you might expect not a single fragrance tested—no matter how putrid—inhibited male arousal.

What's the cheap psychological trick? When it comes to fragrance, less is more. Instead of heading to the cosmetics counter, look to nature to help you elicit the desired response from your mate.

REFERENCES

Hirsch, A. "Smells Really Do Enhance Romance." *Bottom Line Personal* April 15 (1988): 12.
Hirsch, A.R., and A.P. Hirsch. "Scentsational Sex: The Secret to Using Aroma for Arousal." *Element* (1998).

Psychological Strip Poker

Poor communication is one of the most frequent relationship problems. It sounds simple, but conversing with someone is a complicated game. The right kind of communication at the right time is good for you. Too much at the wrong time or in the wrong way is not. Sometimes talk is *not* cheap. To play the game, you've got to know the rules.

Rule No. 1—People talk one at a time, in turns. This is so obvious that it sounds like common sense; however, violate the rule and the talk stops. Other people will walk away from you if you can't play the game, especially in the beginning stages of a relationship. The ability to take turns with small talk is important, but this skill is even more vital when the conversation moves from casual to significant.

Conversational analysts have researched gender and interruption. In a series of studies, males were responsible for 75 percent of the total number of interruptions.

Rule No. 2—Only one person may hold power at a time. Whoever talks most tends to dominate the conversation. Power is determined by the amount of eye contact given to one participant, by the number of interruptions by the would-be power holder, and by the amount of time one person spends talking and laughing.

An interesting aside: Laughter, usually a shared experience, can be an indication of who holds the power in a conversation. One person invites the other to laugh. The one who tells the funny story holds the power; the one who laughs gives in. When someone tries to make you smile or laugh, they're trying to take back the power in the conversation.

Rule No. 3—If for some reason the conversation becomes unbalanced or uncomfortable, order will be reestablished. There are many ways this can happen. Here is one example. During a group conversation, several people may start talking at once or a few may start talking with each other in smaller groups. Participants then feel anxious because they realize they are missing out on others' conversations. Ultimately, everyone will resume taking turns.

Silence is also threatening. If one person pauses for too long (usually around thirty seconds) in the middle of a conversation, other members of the group begin to fidget.

Rule No. 4—"Uhs," "ahs," and "wells" are fair tactics to avoid unpleasantness. Conversation analysts have reaffirmed what psychologists have known for years: Humans will deny pain as long as they can. They will continue with a conversation long after they are ready for it to be over. So when the talk takes a turn you find disagreeable, go ahead and "um" and "ah" for the sake of politeness until you see a graceful way to make your exit. But be careful, too many "ums" can leave the impression that you are being dishonest.

Rule No. 5—Offering too much information—positive or negative—is a turnoff. Talk too much about yourself to casual acquaintances, and they will think you're conceited. Disclose too much about yourself to your partner, and you may be in for trouble. To make sure you don't make this mistake, remember what you learned in the first grade. Take turns. When your partner divulges something positive about himself, offer something positive back about yourself. If your mate discloses something negative about herself, respond with something sympathetic and supportive, perhaps even making a small confession about yourself. But do it gradually. Revealing too much at one time can cause mental overload.

Consider this situation: your mate decides to give you too much information about his or her past. You thought you knew this person, but now you're shocked. You thought you had a lot in common, but now that you've discovered all this, you're scared, defensive, and worried. The relationship will suffer.

People like people who are like them. Too many negative or too many positive revelations may make your mate think, "We're not alike at all." Our human response is to distance ourselves from those we perceive to be too different from us.

What's the cheap psychological trick? If there are serious issues involved, get them out in the open as your relationship starts to develop. It's important to know this kind of information before making the decision to continue a relationship. If both of you decide you want to talk about your past, take turns. Offer one little thing about yourself, and wait for your partner to return with something similar. Raise the stakes slowly, and allow your partner to do the same thing. Think of it as "psychological strip poker." Playing the game this way keeps the relationship in balance. Do it like this, and both of you can discover each other's pasts on equal footing.

REFERENCES

"Boy Meets Girl, Boy Interrupts Girl." *Health* May/June (1990): 11+.

Johnson, K. "Until Death (or 11 Years) Do Us Part." *Kentucky Alumnus* Spring (1997): 12+.

Smells Like Love

You may have heard the expression "Absence makes the heart grow fonder." Well, not always. Sometimes "Out of sight, out of mind" exerts a more powerful sway—especially when temptation is thrown in your absent lover's path. Is there a way to keep your presence alive even when the love of your life is out of sight? Absolutely. Use the sense of smell to your advantage.

Smell is a powerful sense, and it's the only one that has its own special spot in the brain. All other senses go to the hypothalamus before they are routed to their designated part of the brain. Research has suggested that this special smell center is a genetic throwback to the time when it was essential to sense predators through smell. Being able to smell predators long before they could see them helped our prehistoric ancestors survive.

This sense is so compelling that many use it to remember a lost loved one. Widows and widowers tell of going to their dearly departed's closet and smelling their clothing to call up memories and to feel the presence of their loved one just one more time. When the grieving partners come in contact with someone who is wearing the same cologne as their departed mate, the flood of memories may overwhelm them. The sense of smell is so powerful that it can help recover hidden, or in this case, buried memories.

Once upon a time the love letter was an art, and Victorian England took passionate missives to a new level. When sealing a love note, the sender would liberally sprinkle her perfume on the envelope. When the letter was delivered, the recipient's sense of smell informed him that this letter was from his true love before he opened it. No thought involved, just pure response.

This trick works today. It doesn't take a lot of perfume. Our sense of smell is so keen that a wisp of perfume is actually more effective than a dollop. If your loved one is going out of town, slip a little note in his or her luggage with your cologne gently sprayed on the card. Hide the card so you'll also have the element of surprise working for you. Your lover's sense of smell is genetically wired to respond, so you might as well take advantage of it.

What's the cheap psychological trick? Just as an animal marks its territory, you can mark your mate's subconscious with your perfume or cologne. When the scent is detected, a flood of emotions associated with you will surge forth. It's a great way to stay in your lover's mind, even when you are physically far away.

REFERENCE

Banashek, M. "Shorts take." *Psychology Today* 31 (1997): 88.

Cheap Trick No. 10

Mooning
Over You!

True love and full moons go hand in hand in literature and lore. Does the moon bring out the lover in us? Well, it depends on whom you ask. Overall, the answer is a qualified...well, you decide.

The natural satellite that circles our planet approximately once a month has been a source of superstition for thousands of years. The moon has been worshipped and it has been blamed for incomprehensible events. Until fairly recently people believed that too much moon exposure led to madness, hence the word "lunatic," from the Latin word *luna* for moon. Alexander Graham Bell was so convinced that the moon's "magnetic forces" could harm his health that he covered the windows in his home to block out the rays of a full moon.

Most of us no longer really believe that the moon influences our behavior. But research has shown that when the moon exerts its pull, most people grow anxious without knowing why. Being modern, cerebral creatures who dismiss the power of nature over us, most of us automatically look for external causes to explain this anxiety. We assume that this anxiety is the result of the pressures of work, home, or love. In an attempt to feel better, we work harder at making decisions and solving problems, thinking that they are the source of the anxiety. The truth is this anxiety comes and goes as the moon waxes and wanes.

What's the cheap psychological trick? If you're looking for a commitment, then ask for it on a new moon or full moon plus or minus two days. Your would-be mate will be experiencing the pull of the moon and probably won't have a clue where all that anxiety is coming from. He or she will be looking for ways to reduce the anxiety and will be in a good state of mind to make a decision. People are also 30 percent more sexually active during a full moon, so this might be a good time to get lucky!

REFERENCE

Jordan, N. "Mind Over Moon." *Psychology Today* 19 July (1985): 8.

Cheap Trick No. 11

The Name Game

If you're trying to decide who among a group of potential candidates is the mate for you, consider this unusual approach.

Assume that Betty has three beaus. Assume, also, that Betty enjoys their company equally and that each of the three men is equally attractive. Betty must pick the one she likes best. Which one will it be? They seem equal in every conceivable way, but their names are different, and therein lies the key.

Let's say the men are named Allen, Bart, and Charles. Which one will Betty pick? All things being equal, as they are in this example, the winner will most likely be Bart. Why? As strange as it sounds, because his name begins with B and so does Betty's.

Researchers looked at the names of 42,257 married couples. They found a statistically significant number of

28

alliteratively named mates. In other words, similarly named couples occurred more often than would be expected by chance. If you throw in nicknames, there were even more alliterative alignments. The researchers, however, were quick to say this did not predict marital success.

Although no one knows why similar mate monikers attract each other, the general thought is that alliteration appeals to people. The pleasant combination of sounds provides another perceived connection, indirectly tricking the brain into thinking, "He or she is just like me."

What's the cheap psychological trick? When all else fails, and you just can't narrow the field of potential mates, consider their names. You may find it easier to establish a close relationship with someone who shares the first letter of your name.

REFERENCES

Bozzi, Vincent. "Selecting Similar Mate Monikers." *Psychology Today* 19 November (1985): 12.

Kopelman, R.E., and D. Long. "Alliteration in Mate Selection: Does Barbara Marry Barry?" *Psychological Reports* 56 (1985): 791–796.

Age Before Beauty?

Men, imagine a situation in which you could pick either a much younger or a much older wife. Which would you choose? Be careful. There are benefits and drawbacks to each choice.

If you selected the younger wife, here's the good news. Researchers have found that men with younger wives live 13 percent longer.

If you chose an older wife, there's good news as well. According to research, the *quality* of your relationship will be better. Younger men reported that their more senior partner understood them better and had more similar needs and interests—especially sexually. Older wives felt less need to change to conform to marital standards and were not as interested in being pampered as younger women. The researchers found that the majority of these relationships lasted about four to seven years. For some, that was enough happiness for a lifetime.

What's the cheap psychological trick? Men, if you want to live longer, marry a younger woman. Want a happy marriage? Marry an older woman.

The choice is yours.

REFERENCES

Ackerman, D. *A Natural History of Love.* New York: Random House, 1994.

Michael, R.T., J.H Gagnon, E.O. Laumann, and G. Kolata. *Sex in America: A Definitive Survey.* Boston: Little Brown, 1994.

"Older Wives, Better Lives." *Psychology Today* 17 (1984): 12.

"Younger Wives, Longer Lives." *Psychology Today* 17 (1984): 12.

Cheap Trick No. 13

Nature Rules

Finally, an answer to the age-old question: what do women want in a man? Perhaps you think the answer comes from massive psychological research. Not so. Psychologists don't know what a woman wants any more than the rest of us do. To find the answer to this question, we can go back to nature and see what females of other species want.

☀ The American toad, the song sparrow, the meadow katydid, or even the green tree frog are all looking for the same thing—a good singer. The male's call attracts the opposite gender. Men, perhaps you need to work on your conversation skills.

☀ The female Convict cichlid, a tropical fish, will have nothing to do with smaller males. Simply stated, size counts. These fish want a male with a body! Consider a visit to the gym—if you want to attract a Convict cichlid.

☀ The female great titmouse is highly attracted to the male who shows his stripes, strategically emblazoned upon his manly chest. The barn swallow, the crested newt, and the peacock are all looking for a showy tail in their men. And the female red-jungle fowl wants her mate to have an attractive comb. Make sure you're well dressed before you head out on your date.

☀ The female Satin bowerbird looks for the male with the largest and most decorated nest. The bigger the male's love nest, the greater the probability the female will move in. Take a close look at that bach-elor pad if you want to lure a lady to your place.

What's the cheap psychological trick? Look to nature to offer you guidance when you're trying to please a woman.

REFERENCES

Cunningham, M.R., A.R. Roberts, A.P. Barbee, P.B. Druen, and C. Wu. "Their Ideas of Beauty Are, on the Whole, the Same as Ours: Consistency and Variability in the Cross-Cultural Perception of Female Physical Attractiveness." *Journal of Personality and Social Psychology* 68 (1995): 261–279.

Dugartkin, L.A., and J.J. Godin. "How Females Choose Their Mates." *Scientific American* 278 (1998): 56–61.

PART II

Caring
Becoming A Couple

True love is like seeing ghosts. We all talk about it, but few of us have ever seen one.

—*François de la Rochefoucauld*

Brain Gain

Believe it or not, anatomically there's only a 5 percent difference between males and females. If the two genders are 95 percent similar physiologically, why do males and females often find it so difficult to cooperate with one another? Studies in neuropsychology suggest that the answer lies in the anatomy of the brain.

The male brain is 10 to 15 percent bigger than the female brain. However, the regions of the brain responsible for expressive abilities like reading, writing, and parts of language are much smaller in men than in women. When solving problems, women tend to think first and then react. Men are more likely to react immediately and are less willing to stop even when their plans are going awry. This could help to explain why men will *not* ask for directions. A man's smaller frontal lobe may account for his higher tolerance for risk-taking and his reluctance to stop once he's elected a course of action.

The male brain is more compartmentalized or specialized than the female brain. When a female solves a problem, neurons from all over her brain fire and light up like a Christmas tree. When a male solves a problem, one specific part of his brain lights up, significantly more focused than the brains of female problem solvers. Perhaps this helps explain this scenario: A man comes home from a hard day's work, sits down, and tunes out the children, the housework, and the laundry. A woman comes home and immediately starts thinking about everything that must be done.

When a man's brain is not actively engaged in an activity, it idles in the limbic system, a more primitive part of the brain responsible for the expression of aggression and violence. Women's brains idle in a section of the brain called the cingulate gyrus, a more highly evolved part of the brain that is responsible for symbolic expressions, gestures, and words. Now you know why most men do not cuddle after sex. The deed is done, back to reptilian brain idle.

The female's senses are more developed. Her sense of hearing is so keen she can hear a pin drop even when Sprint is not her long-distance phone carrier. The neurons in the brain that regulate how loud things sound are much smaller in men. This helps to explain the male's love of loud music and car racing. The visual cortex in the male brain is bigger, allowing men to respond faster to things they see. The area of the brain that detects and identifies odor is eight times less active in men.

Although men's brains tend to be larger and heavier than women's brains when they are young, the male brain loses tissue about three times as fast as the female brain. By the time people hit their forties, things tend to equal out. A man's brain shrinks so much quicker than a woman's brain that by middle age his incredibly important frontal lobes are close to the same size as the woman's. The result (sorry guys) is poorer memory, a decreasing ability to pay attention, and an increasing tendency toward irritability. Take solace men, women have a three times greater risk for Alzheimer's disease.

Women are far more coordinated than men. Because a male's cerebral cortex has fewer connections, his coordination is weaker than that of a female, whose cerebral cortex is composed of interwoven, overlapping connections.

What's the cheap psychological trick? Recognize that certain differences are physiological, and play to your strengths. Male and female physiologies work best in tandem with each other. This is called complementarity. Your relationship will be stronger and will work more smoothly if you can acknowledge that you need one another. We keep people and things around longer when we perceive a need for them.

REFERENCES

Blum, D. *Sex on the Brain: The Biological Differences Between Men and Women.* New York: Viking, 1997.

Hales, D. "The Female Brain." *Ladies Home Journal* 115 (1998): 128–133.

Kleinwaks, R. "Your Brain." *Men's Health* 14 November (1999): 134.

Tanzi, R.E. "A Promising Animal Model of Alzheimer's Disease." *New England Journal of Medicine* 332 (1995): 1512–1513.

Cheap Trick No. 15

Catch and Release

Assuming you've snared your potential mate, you must now decide if this new "love of your life" is a great catch or a slippery fish you'd be better off throwing back. Don't wait until years into the relationship— deal with this issue now. Divorce courts may take their financial toll, but emotionally damaging breakups may never heal.

When falling in love, you are far too willing to overlook inconsistencies, peculiarities, and other little things which one by one may mean nothing, but added together may indicate something is really screwy. Now's the time to find out if your new lover is playing a cheap psychological trick on *you*, one designed to manipulate your love and keep you constantly off-kilter.

After being with your lover over a period of time, you should be able to predict his or her behavior most of the time. If your mate always keeps you slightly off balance, if you regularly get completely out-of-the-blue reactions to things you do or say—for example, your words of endearment provoke anger—you have been placed on what psychologists call a "variable ratio schedule." Your relationship now has the same payoff schedule as a Vegas slot machine. You keep putting love and affection in, and you never know if you're going to get the cherries or the lemons. Your words or actions may elicit the desired and expected response five times in a row, and then you encounter that unpredictable behavior again! Your lover is manipulating you by keeping you off base, waiting for the big payoff.

If you challenge your unpredictable lover, or threaten to walk out, he or she may sense the loss of control over you and resort to a technique every romantic con knows. It's called "character assassination." You may explain your desire to leave, your unwillingness to comply with a request, then all of a sudden, as if someone threw a switch, your mate hurls expletives at you— massive put-downs, phrases designed to "beat you up" verbally and challenge your worth. This is a powerful trick. In most cases, people who have been made to feel guilty and unworthy will give in and comply with their partner.

Is your lover difficult to pin down psychologically and geographically? Is he gone for unexpected periods of time? Does she often change plans abruptly? Does he hesitate to give you a phone number where you can reach him? Are there fleeting moments when your mate seems to drop a mask and become someone else? Is he or she abusive either physically or verbally? Unpredictable behavior like this is usually the mark of an unstable relationship.

While physical pains can heal quickly, the emotional scars inflicted by an unpredictable lover can last a lifetime. The "Laws of Cognitive Dissonance" are on the side of the romantic con. As long as someone can keep you off balance and as long as you continue to think you can change the undesirable behavior, you'll stick with your capricious mate no matter what.

What's the cheap psychological trick? When you are beginning a relationship, you may be especially vulnerable. Each member of a partnership is entitled to expect a certain amount of reliability and predictability from the other. Learn to recognize manipulative behavior, and don't let your mate grab your emotion and turn off your intellect. If your catch is turning on you, throw that fish back in the sea and bait your hook again.

REFERENCE

Carson, R.C., J.N. Butcher, and S. Mineka. "The Clinical Picture in Antisocial Personality and Psychopathy." *Abnormal Psychology and Modern Life.* New York: Harper Collins College Publishers, 1996, 337–341.

Trust Me?

Trust is a difficult concept to define, yet people throw the word around all the time as if they understand exactly what it means. How often we hear or utter these phrases—the reassuring "You can trust me," the guilt-provoking "Don't you *trust* me?" or the despairing "I don't know if I can trust my lover ever again." Before you use that important word again, consider this.

Recent research suggests that trust—the confidence you feel toward a particular friend, business acquaintance, or life partner—is contingent upon three psychological variables. A person is considered trustworthy when he or she is *predictable, caring,* and *faithful.*

A person earns your trust when he or she exhibits consistent behavior over a period of time. The best predictor of future behavior is past behavior. When you see that someone behaves the same way over and over, after a while you begin to feel comfortable predicting his or her actions, and the level of trust you have for that person grows. Observed consistency, which leads to predictability, forms the foundation necessary in any trusting relationship.

As fledgling trust emerges, you begin to evaluate how caring the other person is. To find out how he or she will respond to your concerns and worries, you must take the initiative, put yourself at risk, and expose your concerns and vulnerabilities. If the other person responds in a caring way consistently over a period of time, you feel free to confide in and rely on him or her, no matter the circumstances. The two of you gradually talk more openly with each other and the relationship grows stronger and stronger. Faith allows you to believe—even when circumstances seem to say otherwise—that another person is truly as good as his or her word. It allows you to believe without question that what you have seen from that person in the past you will also see in the future. When you have faith in someone, you feel certain that he or she will not let you down. Of the three variables of trust, faith in another person is the most closely correlated with the degree of love. The more faith you have in a person, the stronger your love for him or her.

Ironically, when people are asked to define trust, they often forget to list predictability, and they almost never think to include faith.

What's the cheap psychological trick? To ascertain if your lover is truly trustworthy, first determine that his or her actions are predictable (past behaviors predict future behaviors). Second, decide if your lover genuinely cares about you. But finally and most importantly, examine your faith in him or her. In order to build a trusting and loving relationship, two people must believe in one another. An objective—as best you can—analysis of all three gives you an accurate picture of the degree of trust the person deserves.

REFERENCES

Deutsch, F.M., L. Sullivan, C. Sage, and N. Basile. "The Relations among Talking, Liking, and Similarity between Friends." *Personality and Social Psychology Bulletin* 17 (1991): 406–411.

Rempel, J.K., J.G. Holmes, and M.P. Zanna. "Trust in Close Relationships." *Journal of Personality and Social Psychology* 49 (1985): 95–112.

Mama's Boys and Daddy's Girls

What do Douglas MacArthur, Franklin Delano Roosevelt, Harry Truman, and Frank Lloyd Wright all have in common? They were all "mama's boys" (technically called "mammothrepts"). Throughout their lifetimes, these men maintained exceptionally close contact with their mothers. While they led their country's military, presided in the land's highest office, and created architectural masterpieces, they sustained an unusually tight allegiance to their mothers.

At the turn of the twentieth century, Freudian psychoanalysts warned that overprotective mothers could cause serious developmental problems in their sons. In 1942, novelist and social critic Philip Wylie published *Generation of Vipers*, the book that derided and ridiculed the role of mothers and coined the term "momism." Because of Wylie's work, the expression "mama's boy" took on an even more derogatory connotation. To this day, many people believe that a mama's boy is overprotected, spoiled, and unable to think for himself. Consequently, women tend to fear getting involved with a mama's boy.

We could also ask what Pinky MacArthur, Sara Roosevelt, Martha Truman, and Anna Wright have in common. Yes, they were the mothers of the famous mama's boys listed earlier, but they were also daddy's girls, women who had extraordinarily close relationships with their fathers. In an age when women weren't allowed to excel in most fields, these strong women had to sublimate their ambitions; they succeeded vicariously through their famous sons.

The study of "daddy's girls" is a relatively new area of research. Studies indicate that many females who use Dad as a mentor have learned the culturally masculine stereotypes associated with achievement and may have a "leg up" in fields traditionally reserved for men. Perhaps because of this, marrying a daddy's girl can be a threatening event for many men.

Now that you're heading into a relationship with a mama's boy or a daddy's girl, what's the prognosis? The answer isn't as bad as you may have thought. Consider these positive points:

♡ Mama's boys tend to revere their wives more than men who aren't close to their mothers. If he remembers her birthday and calls her regularly, then you too will be the recipient of similar benefits.

♡ When men are accustomed to talking things over with their moms, their communication lines will probably be more open to the other women in their lives, and that includes you.

♡ Mama's boys are lovers of tradition. His mother will go out of her way to keep those traditions alive. As a result, there will be less work for you over the holidays because his mama will do most of it.

♡ Daddy's girls are used to a relationship of equals. In identifying with their fathers, they have learned many of the stereotypical masculine traits and can more easily see things from a male point of view.

♡ Many daddy's girls are flexible. They're into convenience, ease, and simplicity, just like a man.

♡ Daddy's girls aren't as likely to crumble under pressure. They generally know what they want and they're willing to compete for it. They'll manage you in a way that makes sense to you, so why not sit back and enjoy it?

The fact that a daddy's girl chose you suggests that you have many of the qualities she admires in her father.

What's the cheap psychological trick? If you have fallen for a mama's boy or a daddy's girl, don't try to compete. Your best bet is to make friends with your mate's mom or dad. It is to your benefit to work with this bond rather than opposing it. Your relationship with your mate will be stronger if you learn to accommodate these people who are so special in your lover's eyes.

REFERENCES

Maccoby, E. "Gender and Relationships: A Developmental Account." *American Psychologist* 45 (1990): 513–520.

McCullough, D. "Mamma's Boys." *Psychology Today* 17 March (1983): 83–88.

Murphy, B. "Boys to Men: Emotional Miseducation." *The APA Monitor Online* 30 July/August (1999): 1–5.

Wylie, Philip. *Generation of Vipers.* New York: Rinehart and Co., 1942.

Cheap Trick No. 18

How to Win an Argument— Every Time!

What's the most common advice given to new couples? "Never go to bed angry." Good counsel, but tough to achieve. If everyone followed this advice to the letter, there would be a lot more sleepless people out there. Because very few people know how to argue, an ordinary garden-variety discussion can rapidly escalate into a verbal knock-down-drag-out, no-holds-barred fight that goes on for days and is difficult (if not impossible) to forget.

Most of us—unless we were fortunate enough to have had a good debate coach in school—have never been taught the proper technique for arguing. Take a look at the content of daytime talk shows and soap operas. The tears, fights, and melodramatic arguments that produce big ratings teach us the wrong way to argue. Loud, threatening arguments get our adrenalin going and indirectly reinforce negative arguing techniques that are destined to fail. Sadly, parents who argue in front of their children perpetuate this counterproductive cycle of inappropriate arguing. Ninety-nine percent of the time, arguments are a power play—one person trying to control another. But if you're going to argue and win, get your emotions out of the way and forget the petty power plays. If you follow these guidelines, the power will find you.

Sometimes it is better to avoid arguments. Just walk away if you can. But if you must argue, be prepared to go the distance.

When you argue, stick to facts that are impossible to refute and hold your emotions in check. Don't lose sight of the issues at hand. When feelings take over, a discussion can degenerate into an angry confrontation that has very little to do with the points being debated.

Sometimes it's better to stand corrected and end the fight. Don't stubbornly stick to a pig-headed, erroneous stand. If someone disproves your point, acknowledge that you were wrong and get on with your life. Then, throw in the six little words that can smooth over almost any argument and maintain good will: "You're right. I'm wrong. Pardon me."

If today's argument is going nowhere, suggest tabling the argument and set up a time to continue it later. The passage of time may allow both parties to see the issues being discussed more rationally. If you're lucky, a little time will cause memory decay and you won't even remember what you were arguing about.

What's the cheap psychological trick? Argue if you must, but base the argument solely on the facts and don't dig in your heels if you're wrong. Never allow an argument to drag on. Instead, call a truce and continue the discussion later.

As Oscar Wilde, playwright and philosopher, put it, "Arguments are to be avoided. They are always vulgar and rarely convincing."

REFERENCE

Berkowitz, L. *Aggression: Its causes, consequences, and control.* New York: McGraw-Hill, 1993.

Cheap Trick No. 19

Time Out

Reverse psychology can easily backfire on the person who is using it to manipulate someone, but at times in almost every relationship a certain measure of "responsible manipulation" can be healthy and productive.

Suppose you are committed to a relationship, but you feel that your lover is less interested in the liaison than you are. Because your partner seems less committed, you feel compelled to work for love and attention. When your efforts bring about no change, you work even harder. Thinking that you can earn your partner's love, you do everything for him or her. You buy gifts and flowers, send cards (80 percent are bought by women), plan exciting and romantic evenings, show him or her every good time you can dream up, including any number of creative affectionate gestures, indulging your lover's every whim. The more you do, the less response you get. The less response you get, the more you do. Obviously the balance in your relationship is way off-kilter. If you are having to work much harder than your significant other to maintain the relationship, understanding the following concept can help you restore the equilibrium.

The partner who is less involved or less interested holds most of the power in a relationship. The more interested party, the partner who is constantly seeking something, is devalued. The one who is able to grant the favors may even choose to delay the other person's gratification, just to show who's in control. The technical term for this phenomenon is the "Principle of Least Interest." It's nothing new. Long before psychologists described this principle, Socrates, Ovid, Terrence, and Nietzsche wrote about it. Even the *Kama Sutra* acknowledged its power.

Research has shown that when a man is less involved in a relationship, he has the say approximately 70 percent of the time. When a woman is the less involved partner, she wields the power about 50 percent of the time. Whether you are male or female, you may eventually feel that you are doing more than your share to keep the relationship alive. When you reach that point, try this cheap psychological trick.

First, remember an old adage "What's good for the goose is good for the gander." Invoke the principle of least interest on your behalf. Mimic the behavior of the least involved. Back off physically, but not mentally. You know that you want the relationship to grow, but you need to change your obvious tactics. Continue to show some interest in the relationship, but back off on the flowers, calls, cards, romantic stuff in general, and be more frugal with the words "I love you." As you back off, however, you must remain somehow in sight. When your partner is less committed to the relationship than you are, out of sight may truly be out of mind.

One exaggerated way to implement the principle of least interest is the "silent treatment." Twenty-one percent of the people interviewed in a research project admitted using this technique regularly to show their disapproval of their partner's behavior, and they found that it often brought results in one day.

Another application of this principle is withholding sexual privileges. Not smart. This extreme measure can cause more problems than it solves. If the withholding of attention or affection becomes a mere game, or if it becomes a substitute for honest communication, it may backfire like other reverse psychological techniques.

What's the cheap psychological trick? If your partner is constantly taking and never giving—in other words, is expressing "least interest" in you—stop working overtime to earn his or her regard. Slow down on the attention and back off the obvious affectionate gestures for a while. Take back some of the control and restore the balance in the relationship.

REFERENCE
"Not Married—and not Interested." *Psychology Today* 31 March/April (1998): 19.

Cheap Trick No. 20

Easy Doze It!

Many a relationship breaks up over money problems or sexual difficulties. Some researchers, however, now propose that sleep style—specifically snoring—is one of the most common causes of strife between couples. Today, medical practices devoted solely to resolving this noisy problem—from her wheezes to his freight-train rumble—are a growing and thriving business.

Researchers do not know why people snore. Why one person snores on some nights and not on others or at different times in a single night is equally a mystery. They do know that snoring is involuntary and that it stops upon waking. Snorers are unable to hear themselves snore, but anyone else in the room is well aware of those discordant notes, whose volume averages between 60 and 80 decibels. For comparison, a normal conversation ranges from 50 to

70 decibels, a pneumatic drill measures 70 to 90 decibels, and a New York subway averages around 115 decibels. Simply stated, snoring is loud, annoying, and sometimes embarrassing.

Observational statistics inform that 45 percent of normal subjects occasionally snore, and 25 percent are habitual snorers. Snoring becomes more frequent as people age. Recent research has found that there's more to snoring than just the potential to end a relationship. In addition to interrupting healthy sleep patterns that help the body replenish its vital immune system, snoring can also cause problems such as severe headaches, laryngitis, and hearing loss (imagine listening to a pneumatic drill for eight hours).

If you sleep with a snorer, you obviously suffer from "secondhand snoring." You may look upon bedtime as a contest, a race against time to get to sleep before your snoring mate. No doubt you've tried any number of anti-snoring strategies—from waking the snorer to piling pillows over your head, from earplugs to a white noise generator—in hopes of returning peace and quiet to your bedroom. You may have even resorted to *separate* bedrooms.

Sleeping with a snorer not only produces frustration for the sleep-deprived mate, it can also produce irritation and resentment. The techniques described above are only partially effective because none of them reduces that anger, which is often redirected toward the snorer. When you realize that all your efforts have produced mere short-term victories in the war against the snoring, you probably feel

defeated. The harder you try to quell the snoring, the more infuriated you become.

What's the cheap psychological trick? Don't let your anger be misplaced or misdirected. Keep in mind that your beloved mate does not snore intentionally. If you catch yourself growing angry, have a chat with yourself, rethink the issue, and redirect your anger toward solutions.

Ask your snoring spouse for at least an hour's head start at bedtime. Maybe with an extra hour you'll be able to fall asleep before the freight train pulls into the station.

Encourage your partner to keep his or her mouth shut—good advice for most situations, and certainly appropriate in this one. Encourage him to sleep on his side rather than his back—you can even sew tennis balls into the back of his pajama top so that he cannot sleep comfortably on his back.

Try the "barrier technique." Snuggle a wall of pillows between you and your snoring mate. Nuzzling a pillow tightly under or next to your partner also helps to keep her on her side or stomach.

Go to bed together a bit early, cuddle a while, and then retire to another room. When you wake up the next morning—after a refreshing good night's sleep—hop back in bed with your partner for another snuggle.

If all else fails, seek professional help. Every major city has a hospital with a sleep disorders clinic. You may never have thought about it, but sleep—especially snoring—has become big business. These facilities have techniques which range from medications like nose drops to surgical procedures which many insurance companies will reimburse.

REFERENCE

Strollo, P.J., and R.M. Rogers. "Obstructive Sleep Apnea." *New England Journal of Medicine* 334 (1996): 99–104.

Cheap Trick No. 21

Mad For You

When an argument between two people in a close relationship has escalated into an angry confrontation, sticking to the facts, admitting you are wrong, or even giving in to the other person's demands may only bring on another outburst of rage. If you can master a simple technique, you can cut through the anger and get to the real source of the problem.

Keep your emotional cool and listen intently. After your mate has wound down, say this: "Tell me again what's bothering you." Ask only for simple clarification, and, if possible, end the argument on the basis of that answer. When the argument is over, promise to do better, to try harder, and apologize for all your inadequacies and wrongdoings that have been pointed out in the course of the discussion.

After your distraught lover has calmed down, ask gently, "Is there anything else that's bothering you?

Anger, while quite real, is considered to be a "secondary" or "masking" emotion. It tends to cover up what's really going on. As a general rule, the first time people tell you why they're angry and what they want done about it, the words may sound plausible, but they may not reveal the real or original source of the anger. Ask a second time, and the actual root of the anger may come to the surface.

As your partner is winding down from the initial burst of anger and has told you what's bothering him or her, it's smart to ask, "Is there anything else bothering you?" The answer you hear after this second inquiry is the likely to be the source of the real anger. Now, try to remedy that problem, and your lover will believe that you're one-in-a-million because you truly understand.

What's the cheap psychological trick? To get to the root of your lover's anger, first ask, "What's bothering you?" Listen intently; then after the argument settles down—but before the argument is officially concluded—in a sincere voice ask the magic question, "Is there anything *else* bothering you?" The issues brought up in response to the second question are probably the real source of the anger and must be addressed promptly. (Do *not* ask this question a third time or the angry party will think you're being sarcastic.)

REFERENCE

Berkowitz, L. *Aggression: Its causes, consequences, and control.* New York: McGraw-Hill, 1993.

Heart to Heart Talks

Actuarial tables prove that women live about six years longer than their male counterparts. Why the longer life span? One answer may be the female's ability to express emotions.

Early on, most parents start admonishing tearful little boys, telling them "Little boys don't cry." On the other hand, many parents encourage little girls to cry as much as they want. It is far more socially acceptable for women to shed tears than it is for men. It takes very little conditioning to inculcate in little boys the idea that emotions are not their province. Somewhere along the way many men pick up the notion that it is also unmanly even to talk about his feelings. This inappropriate education has now produced a condition called the "John Wayne syndrome."

All bravado and no emotion takes its toll on little John. This learned gender role eventually gets males in trouble.

Men are four times more likely to be involved in a homicide than women. Men ignore the warning signs of illness. Bigger risk takers and far more aggressive drivers, they are more likely to die in an automobile accident. Because a man holds in his emotions, he increases his chance of heart disease.

When asked to list human emotions (there are approximately 750), males generally speak of six—angry, tense, anxious, upset, sexually wanting, or fine. It is socially acceptable for grown men to cry on only two occasions: (1) when a loved one dies, and (2) when their favorite team loses in a major athletic competition.

Assuming you want to keep the love of your life around for a long time, you'd better start now helping him vent those emotions. Behind every bigger-than-life John Wayne alter ego is a down-to-earth, everyday Marion Michael Morrison (John Wayne's real name) who has a need to express emotions and communicate.

What's the cheap psychological trick? Help your partner vent his emotions.

♡ *Make him cry.* Send him flowers. Take him to funerals. Rent macho movies with adult emotional themes. Put *Beaches* back on the shelf and pick up *Saving Private Ryan* or *Brian's Song.* In the privacy of his own home, your man's emotions can sally forth in a safe environment. For his ego's sake, make sure the lights are on low! And don't worry about putting tissue out. He'll use his sleeve instead.

♡ *Make him play.* Kidnap him on three-day vacations. Many men tend to sublimate their troubles into work. This hard-working man believes that he is absolutely integral, essential to the corporate world, so he takes little time off. He might, however, take a short vacation now and then. Get him away from his beepers and cell phone. Treat him to a massage.

♡ *Get him walking.* Walk around the neighborhood with the love of your life for ten to twenty minutes each day and help him reduce some of those pressure-cooker stressors.

♡ *Get him talking.* Ask open-ended questions about specific actions and behaviors. If you ask "Did you have a nice day today, dear?" you'll get the standard, "Uh-huh." (That question works beautifully if a female is your mate. They take that question as a signal to tell you everything.)

REFERENCE

Williams III, G. "John Wayne Disease: Strong, Silent Types are Weak on Life Expectancy." *Longevity* 5 March (1993): 60.

Cheap Trick No. 23

Waltzing Through Life

Arthur Murray had it right. It is absolutely possible to dance away your blues. Since ballroom dancing is back in style and growing in popularity, a lot of couples out there are inadvertently practicing a cheap psychological trick designed to enhance their relationship.

Research suggests that physically exercising with another person increases one's passion for that individual. The attraction may arise from some principle of primitive biology having to do with sweat and pheromones, but that's not the point of this trick. However, you might want to make a mental note concerning the possibility of increased amorousness after strenuous exercise with your partner.

Dancing is an excellent form of exercise, and exercise is good for you. But that's not the point of this trick either. When you dance with your partner, you are doing much more than exercising your muscles, you are strengthening the bond that holds you together. A dancing couple is locked in the same fun step. You're doing the same thing at the same time.

When you take your partner onto the dance floor, you look at each other. Research clearly shows that when two people are in love, they look at each other in a different way. Couples who have been together for a long time often forget to really look at each other. Gazing into one another's eyes during dancing reminds you of your devotion to each other.

When you are dancing, you are alone with your mate. You may be in a room with hundred fellow dancers, but while you're locked in your lover's arms, well, that's all that matters.

When engaged in terpsichorean delight, you're lost in your thoughts. Family, work, and personal worries can drift away, and you become trapped in a "flow state." This term may be new to you, but sports fans will understand the concept. Athletes regularly speak of—even hope and pray for—flow states. When they are "trapped in the zone," time stands still—and well it should for those individuals in love.

Dancing exercises your heart, both literally and figuratively. The movement is good for you physiologically, but it is also psychologically and romantically beneficial. Dancing together lets you show your love for each other.

What's the cheap psychological trick? Face the music and dance! To move your relationship to a deeper level, invite your partner onto the dance floor. Locked in a beautiful step, you will waltz through life together. Dancing is not only good for the mind and heart, it also tricks two people into working together, even if it is for a brief two-step.

REFERENCE

Csikszentimihalyi, M. *Creativity: Flow and the Psychology of Discovery and Invention.* New York: Harper Collins, 1996.

Cheap Trick No. 24

How Do I Love Thee?

When it comes to romance, men and women are not from competing planets. Surveys have shown that males and females both want the same thing from an intimate relationship—a closer emotional rapport. Both genders see sex as a way to heighten this harmony and ultimate unity. But males focus more on the "means," and females focus more on the "end."

Men think that the sexual act is the *means* to finding rapport with their partner.

Women think that the sexual act is *proof* of it.

This strange quirk of human nature pits one gender against the other in sexual situations. If you want to enhance your rapport with your partner, forget about the sexual act for a moment and think about learning to communicate. Improve your communication and improve your relationship. Find a variety of ways to show your affection for your mate.

♡ Let your partner know what makes you feel good.

♡ Say "I love you" as often as you think of it.

♡ Give your lover a little "nothing" gift—not necessarily an expensive one—when it's least expected.

♡ Swap roles around the house one day a month.

♡ If your mate loves rugby, learn the game. If your lover likes to dance, take a ballroom dancing class together. (You get the idea.)

♡ If something your mate does bothers you, especially if it is genuinely deleterious to the relationship, approach the subject gently and discuss it in a safe environment. Come up with a workable plan both of you can live with. Perfect the art of compromise.

♡ Get to know your lover's friends.

♡ Every day come up with a new reason for loving your partner. Designate a special moment during the day—over breakfast or just before bedtime—for you and your mate to exchange the new reasons for loving one another you have discovered. Make it routine. Don't skip a day. After fifty years you will accumulate 18,250 reasons why you belong together.

What's the cheap psychological trick? To build rapport between you and your mate, borrow a line from Elizabeth Barrett Browning and ask the question, "How do I love thee? Let me count the ways." People who regularly count their blessings tend to live longer, happier, and healthier lives. Couples who regularly review the reasons they are attracted to each other stay together longer.

REFERENCE

Levenson, R.W., L.L. Carstensen, and J. M. Gottman. "Long-Term Marriage: Age, Gender, and Satisfaction." *Psychology and Aging* 8 (1993): 301–313.

For Better or Perhaps Worse

Now that you've snared a potential mate, the fun's just starting. Making a relationship last a lifetime is a tall order. How are you going to keep each other happy for the next fifty years? What are the odds of this match made in heaven lasting until that golden anniversary? Are there some predictors that can give you an idea about how durable your partnership will be?

No one can offer guarantees, but according to research, if you grew up in a family where Mom and Dad were both present, where they communicated openly and freely, and showed their love and affection one for another, your relationship—and marriage, if that is on the agenda—will have a greater chance of success and longevity. If you grew up in a broken home or in a single-parent home you may have to work harder. Talk with people whose relationships have stood the test of time. It's never too late to learn. If you have known your prospective mate for a long time and if your finances are secure, your partnership has an even better chance of lasting. Mature people who consider themselves to be relatively happy tend to have longer, healthier relationships than people who are often depressed and who look to others for happiness.

What's the cheap psychological trick? Know your odds of success in advance and approach the relationship wide-eyed and honestly. Use these predictors as guidelines and stay together for a lifetime.

REFERENCES

Kenrick, D.T., S.L. Neuberg., K.L. Zierk, and J.M. Krones. "Evolution and Social Cognition: Contrast Effects as a Function of Sex, Dominance, and Physical Attractiveness." *Personality and Social Psychology Bulletin* 20 (1994): 210–217.

Kenrick, D.T., E.K. Sadalla, G.R. Groth, and M.R. Trost. "Evolution, Traits, and the Stages of Human Courtship: Qualifying the Parental Investment Model." *Journal of Personality* 58 (1990): 97–117.

A Little
Touched

What did Fred and Wilma Flintstone know that Lucy and Desi didn't? Why were Herman and Lily Munster more "with it" than Ward and June Cleaver? Why is ballroom dancing superior to line dancing? What does the European style of kissing have over the American method? How do spiritual healers do what they do?

What's the common denominator? It's all in the touch.

When children are young, the culture allows them to touch and touch often. Good parents show their affection toward their children by frequent touching and holding. Then when children hit adolescence the amount of touching—once freely accepted and given—gradually tapers off. Every elementary school teacher knows that students respond lovingly to touch during the early years of their schooling, but when puberty kicks in, so do any number of rational and irrational fears, and the touching is curtailed. While dating, couples touch each other lovingly. Then as the relationship continues over months and years, touch slows down and in many cases, stops altogether.

Our need for touch does not diminish. Why do we stop touching? Humans crave touch, but today the slightest pat on the shoulder is shunned in the workplace for fear of a lawsuit. No wonder the massage business is thriving. People now pay for touch in a world where once upon a time an affectionate touch between friends and family was the norm.

Every psychology 101 student knows the research on touching. Patrons who have received a gentle pat from the librarian as they check out a book consistently give that library a more favorable rating. Used car salespeople who casually—so lightly it's almost not perceived—touch their customers have a greater chance of making the sale. There is power in a touch.

The Flintstones and the Munsters were the first married couples in television history to sleep in the same bed. Some researchers believe that sleeping together is essential for marriage growth. Initial findings suggest that a couple who sleeps together night after night indirectly synchronize their biological and magnetic waves and cycles. It could happen. Even female college freshmen who live together in a dormitory often find that their monthly menstrual cycles become synchronized. It takes only a few days for newborn babies to match their heartbeats to that of

their parents. Certainly sleeping together and touching for at least seven hours a night must be a powerful bonding force.

Which is better for you, one kiss on each cheek or one kiss on the mouth? If you have a choice, take one kiss on each cheek and get twice the stimulation. The European style of kissing activates both sides of the brain. A kiss on the left cheek stimulates the right side of the brain; a little buss on the right activates the left side of the brain.

Then there's the healing touch. From Russian research of the early twentieth century to modern-day psychological experiments, the research is clear. A simple touch can be healing. Physicians who touch their patients in a "gracious, nonsexual, loving way" increase the speed with which their patients heal. Touching informs a sick person that someone cares about them.

What's the cheap psychological trick? Touch often. Couples who touch increase the probability of celebrating their seventy-fifth anniversary.

And when people you love are ill, touch them and visualize their health restored. You'll never know if you have the healing touch if you don't try.

REFERENCES

Borelli, M., and P. Heidt (Eds). *Therapeutic Touch: A Book of Readings.* New York: Springer Publishing Co., 1981.

Guerro, L.K., and P.A. Andersen. "Patterns of Matching and Initiation: Touch Behaviour and Touch Avoidance across Romantic Relationship States." *Journal of Nonverbal Behavior* 18 (1994): 137–153.

Cheap Trick No. 27

The Big Zero

You've been a couple for a while now. Some of you are married. Things seem to be going well, but you just want to be on top of things as your relationship matures. Are there certain periods when you should particularly be on guard?

Marriage counselors and divorce lawyers have always held that the first, fifth, and ninth years are the most difficult for married couples. The reasons the first year is hard are obvious—adjusting to living with each other, getting used to new responsibilities, coordinating your schedules.

The fifth year is a bit trickier. By now you've worked through initial compatibility issues. But about this time, thoughts of family kick in, and with those thoughts come worries about added responsibilities and fears of failure. If either partner has doubts about the relationship, the logical decision at this point may be "Get out now, before children enter the equation."

The ninth year leads up the first "Big Zero" in the marriage, the tenth anniversary. This is a major milestone in any relationship. "Big 0" anniversaries, whether the tenth, twentieth or fiftieth, are natural times for reflection. They are occasions for assessing accomplishments and failures. The tenth anniversary is also a natural "jumping-off point." Some may see this as the logical time to call it quits and to start the search for another more compatible mate before it is too late.

What's the cheap psychological trick? Be especially vigilant on those special anniversaries and use them as occasions for positive reevaluation of your relationship and as times for solving problems that may have arisen in your years together.

REFERENCE

Kenrick, D.T., S. Neuberg, K. Zierk, and J. Krones. "Evolution and social cognition: Contrast effects as a function of sex, dominance, and physical attractiveness." *Personality and Social Psychology Bulletin,* 20 (1994): 210–217.

Levenson, R.W., L.L. Carstensen, and J.M. Gottman. "Long-term marriage: Age, gender, and satisfaction." *Psychology and Aging,* 8 (1993): 301–313.

 # PART III

 ## Pairing

Getting It on Together

That was the most fun I've
ever had without laughing.

—Woody Allen

Cheap Trick No. 28

Dining In

After lovemaking, females crave attention and men often just want to go home or to sleep. Is there a way to satisfy both parties' needs?

One thing that men and women have in common after expressing their love is hunger. Sexual activity is an aerobic activity, and it burns calories. No doubt you remember from ninth grade biology that your body converts food into sugar and then uses it for fuel. During lovemaking, your muscles use that sugar and your blood-sugar levels go down. This triggers a signal that you need food.

After sexual activity, enjoy a little snack while lounging in bed. Women achieve their goal of keeping their men in bed just a little longer, and men satisfy their need to do something else—anything else—after sex. Dining in bed keeps both of you communicating and tightens those relationship bonds.

What's the cheap psychological trick? Maybe the way to a man's heart is through his stomach, especially after sex. To keep your partner around longer, have the fast food ready so he won't make a fast dash outta there!

REFERENCE

Rathus, S.A., J.S. Nevid, and L. Fichner-Rathus. *Human Sexuality in a World of Diversity.* Boston: Allyn & Bacon, 1997.

Remember My Name

Would you like to control what's going on your mate's head when the two of you are making love? Well, you can—for a little while at least. Use the technique described in the previous trick and engage in a little mind control.

At some point in every relationship, one member of the couple has wondered what the other is thinking about during sex. You probably hope that you are the center of those thoughts. Of course, if your partner calls out the wrong name, you have an answer you'll never forget. To keep this from ever happening, exert a little control. First, remember the classical conditioning rule. Two things must come together—one of them must be an automatic body function, like sexual behavior, and the other can be any outside stimulus. Here's how to turn this into "mind control"—for a little while, at least.

What's the cheap psychological trick? When your partner is at the point of no return, the point where the automatic orgasmic response has kicked in, make this simple demand: "Call my name." Even in the throes of physical passion, repeat this request. Then if you really want to get creative, say, "Tell me you love me."

Look what's going on. You've associated your name with sexual pleasure and with love. Now when your mate thinks of your name, a little mental Viagara will kick in.

REFERENCE

Pavlov, I. *Conditioned Reflexes: An Investigation of the Physiological Activity of the Cerebral Cortex.* London: Oxford University Press, 1927.

Cheap Trick No. 30

Love
Slave

Sexual behavior is one of those things that seems to have a mind of its own. Some aspects of the sex act involve the autonomic—or involuntary—nervous system. As a result, sexual behavior can be conditioned, often without the individual even being aware of it.

When an automatic body function, like sexual behavior, occurs simultaneously—or almost simultaneously—with any particular stimulus, the two things become associated in a person's mind. For instance, imagine that you are in the throes of orgasmic delight and the telephone rings. The next day at the office, you might find yourself sexually excited when you hear the phone ring. To get your work done, you may need to take the phone off the hook. The stimulus could be anything—a thunderclap, a smell, a song, a piece of clothing. Once that stimulus becomes associated with a special sexual event, it's a sexual aid.

Want to improve your partner's sexual performance? Pick a special stimulus. Then at the point of sexual no return, when your partner's climax is inevitable, turn on that music, light that scented candle—get your stimulus working. It will now be paired autonomically with sexual pleasure. You've now created a sexual love slave—one conditioned to think of sex and salivate accordingly when that sexual stimulus makes its next appearance.

Careful. It is possible to condition people so well that they believe they cannot function without the stimulus. Maybe you'd better come up with a new stimulus from time to time!

If you choose food for your stimulus, don't pick your mate's absolute favorite—Choose an appealing food, but something you don't eat regularly. An item that's too common will have your partner thinking about sex every time that food appears—no matter where or when—and the trick will lose its potency.

What's the cheap psychological trick? With the appropriate stimulus, it is possible to rise to the occasion. How powerful is this trick? It really doesn't matter. If you've gone out of your way to prepare the boudoir for this special occasion, your partner is going to be impressed with all the attention, and that might be all you need to get started. May the force be with you.

REFERENCE

Pavlov, I. *Conditioned Reflexes: An Investigation of the Physiological Activity of the Cerebral Cortex.* London: Oxford University Press, 1927.

Cheap Trick No. 31

Love Salad

From cantharides (Spanish fly) to yohimbine, from oysters to ground-up yak horn, from amyl nitrite to alcohol, men and women have searched for the perfect aphrodisiac. Many chemical aphrodisiacs work because they reduce human inhibitions and increase the willingness to respond in previously unaccepted ways. Actually, you can make your own aphrodisiac. Just take a look in your kitchen cupboard. In fact, you may find that a new twist will help a few familiar ingredients enhance your lovemaking. Pick one from the list below that's fairly benign, and then apply the cheap psychological trick.

✴ *Tomatoes*. The French call tomatoes *pommes d'amour* or "love apples" and claim they have qualities that can take anyone's lovemaking to new heights. (Also, stewed tomatoes are not just delicious, they're also good for your male lover's prostate.)

✢ *Oranges*. These golden orbs were treasured by the Greeks as food for the gods, and you know the Greek gods were a lustful lot.

✢ *Chocolate*. The Aztec emperor Montezuma consumed sixteen flagons of a rich cocoa elixir each day before entering his harem.

✢ *Vanilla*. When Cortes went back to Europe after conquering the Aztec empire, he took chocolate and vanilla, mixed the two, and an aphrodisiac was born. Thomas Jefferson was so taken with this new concoction he had it shipped from Paris to Monticello.

The sex act is both physical and mental. Here's how to make both parts work for you.

✷ Start with a big serving of the aphrodisiac of your choice. Make sure that the bowl of strawberries, for instance, is placed in a prominent place in the room. Use it as an actor would use a prop. Give it a story, explain its history, play it up.

✷ Offer it with a tease. Of course, you're going to share, but half the fun of this placebo is in the tease. Pretend to offer your aphrodisiac, then take it away. Repeat until you have your lover eating out of the palm of your hand.

✷ Demonstrate its aphrodisiacal properties. When you behave as if you are turned on by its valuable love chemicals, your partner will begin to mirror your behavior. The next thing you know, he or she is more aroused from watching you than from your aphrodisiac. The brain doesn't know or care where the arousal is coming from.

What's the cheap psychological trick? If you behave as if an aphrodisiac is working on you, it will work wonders for your partner.

REFERENCE

Rathus, S.A. "The Placebo Effect," *Psychology in the New Millennium*. Fort Worth, Texas: Harcourt Brace College Publishers, 1999.

Precious Moments

When are you at your sexiest? Are there special times of the day when your randy nature takes over and you have a need for love? Can you think of moments in the day when your physical relationship with your lover seems more meaningful? A recent survey in *New Woman* magazine listed those times of day when people say they feel sexy. Interestingly enough, men and women agreed on most moments—but then men think anytime is a good time for sex. Here are those special, opportune moments.

Special Times	Women	Men
After a shower/bath	35%	25%
On vacation	12%	11%
After a few drinks	12%	10%

After working out	11%	17%
After sex	8%	6%
At bedtime	8%	10%
In the morning	6%	8%
After dinner	3%	3%
Other times/Don't know	5%	10%

According to this survey, only 6 percent of women and 8 percent of men are aware of the biologically ideal time for sex.

The human body clock is so powerful that if you were born at four o'clock in the morning, it's likely that you'll die at four o'clock in the morning. Researchers estimate that the average person goes through many chemical cycles—and hence has many different cravings—in one twenty-four period, all regulated by this incredibly precise biological clock.

According to your biological clock, the correct time for sexual activity is early in the morning, between six and eight in the morning. This is probably a throwback to prehistoric times. When a mate left the cave thousands of years ago, there was no guarantee that he or she would be back later that day. Back when there truly was a need to populate the earth and maintain the tribe, the biological clock instinctively kicked in early in the morning. As it rang "wake up," it also gave humans the urge to procreate. Then, if the male was eaten by a saber-toothed tiger, at least his seeds had been sown before he left the cave that morning, and the probability was higher that the tribe's number would increase.

What's the cheap psychological trick? The other sexy times listed above are nice, but early morning is a guaranteed sexy moment. So, instead of hurrying off to be stuck in traffic, take an extra moment and express your affection physically for the love of your life. Trust me. It'll make the drive into work much more palatable.

REFERENCES

Hopkins, K. "Clock Setting." *Scientific American* 278 April (1998): 20–22.

Moore-Ede, M.C., F.M. Sulzman, and C.A. Fuller. *The Clock That Times Us.* Cambridge, MA: Harvard University Press, 1982.

"Those sexy moments." *New Woman* April (1998): 20.

Cheap Trick No. 33

Sex Is Good For You

Researchers have found that approximately one in four people found relief from headaches after sex. Why? No one has a clue. Perhaps it's as simple as distracting one's attention from pain and turning it toward pleasure. Another possible explanation is that sex releases the body's natural painkillers, our endogenous morphines called endorphins. One other possible explanation is that some forms of foreplay may involve a degree of massage; stroking, gentle kneading, and manipulating skin tissue from head to toe is relaxing and pleasurable in and of itself. The response is not specific to the one area massaged, but is generalized all over the body, unwinding constricted muscles.

Even better news: sex will help with more than a headache:

✴ The Heart. Increased heart rate during periods of lovemaking strengthens heart muscle and improves the circulation.

✴ Immune System. Sexual activity increases hormone output. Both estrogen and testosterone levels increase; these hormones work with other systems to fortify cell immunity.

✴ Cholesterol. It is believed that sexual activity releases another hormone, DHEA, which reduces body fat and cholesterol.

✴ Stress. Touching between lovers reduces anxiety and stress.

What's the cheap psychological trick? Safe, responsible sex can be good for what ails you.

REFERENCES

Blanchard, E.B. "Psychological Treatment of Benign Headache Disorders." *Journal of Consulting & Clinical Psychology* 60 (1992): 537–551.

Cohen, S., D.A. Tyrrell, and A.P. Smith. "Negative Life Events, Perceived Stress, Negative Affect, and Susceptibility to the Common Cold. *Journal of Personality & Social Psychology* 64 (1993): 131–140.

Ukestad, L.K., and D.A. Whittrock. "Pain Perception and Coping in Female Tension Headache Sufferers and Headache-Free Controls. *Health Psychology* 15 (1996): 65–68.

"Yes, tonight, dear. I have a headache." *Men's Health* 4 (1988): 10.

Take A Bath

You've had a hard day at work. You're tired, irritable, and just plain unhappy. Your loving mate greets you at the door and asks, "Did you have a nice day?" The next thing you know, insults are flying, tension is magnified times ten, anger is raging, even the family pet is barking unhappily. You storm off to your room, mentally visualize the scene over and over, exaggerating it out of proportion. Or you go through the motions of family life—dining, watching television, attempting chitchat. Even though no one has said a cross word, hours later there's still tension in the air.

Want to improve your relationship with your mate? Easy. Come in the front door, acknowledge to your partner "I'm home," then head straight upstairs and take a bath. Just you in the shower or tub with your nice scented soap—your favorite loofah and tubby toy are optional. Just let the water cascade off your body, and magically the day's troubles float away. When you are done, hopefully the worries will go down the drain.

This trick is powerful, but very few people use it. Although the Romans knew the wonders of the bath, most modern gladiators dismiss it as too elementary, too simple, too easy. Most people haven't a clue—outside of "happy hour"—how to unwind after a day of stresses and strains. That's why happy hour is so popular. Not because the alcohol is so tasty, but because it serves as a central nervous system depressant, which chemically turns down the harsh glare of the day. A good warm bath will do the same thing; it's cheaper and has few to no negative side effects. Here's why this trick works.

✵ The bath serves as down time, putting distance between you and your mate until you've had time to wash the office out of your head.

✵ The smell of the bath is chemically different from the smells you've been used to all day long. This indirectly signals to the brain that you're in a different place and ready to unwind.

✵ Scrubbing is a ritualistic way to feel that you're removing the taint of the workplace.

✵ The heat from the bath unwinds tight muscles, raises body temperature, and calms you down.

What's the cheap psychological trick? Taking a bath is a ritual way to cleanse yourself from your dirty job, a physical way to relax, and a distancing technique which offers you time to count to ten before you take out your misplaced hostility on your mate.

REFERENCE

Black, I.B. *Information in the Brain: A Molecular Perspective.* Cambridge, MA: MIT Press, 1991.

Cheap Trick No. 35

Sex Manuals

Some of the best selling books in the 1900s were marriage manuals. You might assume that because they were published during the Victorian Era they are prudish and priggish. You may think that these books—because they were written at a time when women were required to feign a fainting spell at the mere hint of an obscenity—skirt the issues. Not so. These manuals featured very explicit sexual instructions. They were bought by men and women alike, and they achieved bestseller status in their day.

Although these books fell out of favor for a while, the genre is now flourishing and it is more graphic than ever. You don't have to look far to find any number of books, videos, and all kinds of sexual toys that promise to put the zip back into your sex life.

An entire industry has been built on the modern romance novel. While they may not look like sex manuals of yore, these steamy publications serve as sexual horn books for much of the population. Don't knock it till you try it— something must be working. After all, people who read romance novels report both having and enjoying sex more often than those who read the stock market report.

What's the cheap psychological trick? If sexual manuals—or the sexual aid of your choice—give your lovemaking a boost, go for it. Sex on the brain translates to sex in the physical world, and good sex can be one powerful bond in any relationship.

REFERENCE

Oliver, A. *Finishing Touches, A Guide to Being Poised, Polished, and Beautifully Prepared for Life.* New York: Bantam Books, 1990.

A Passion For Sports, or Touchdown!

Football widows—those who can't get their partner's attention when anything sports related is on TV—will be pleased to know that there is a way to use sports to your sexual advantage! Imagine a typical weekend day when your loving mate is seated comfortably in his recliner, sipping his favorite beverage, and eating curly chemical cheese products. Hypnotized by the screen, he may not notice you even if you parade around naked. Don't try it; don't even think about it; and don't worry that they prefer watching men parade around in tight pants. This is a cheap trick for after the game.

Remember that the part of the male brain that's responsible for aggression also controls sexual arousal. Use this to your advantage. To say that your mate is charged up after the game is an understatement—even if his team lost. At the end of the game, this part of his brain is ready to work, either aggressively or sexually, in overtime. Just make sure at the end of the game you show up in his favorite team's jersey. This simple change of apparel will move your spouse from sports action to sexual play.

The technical name for this trick is "sexual excitation transfer," and it can work just about anytime. Planning a honeymoon or hoping for a love-filled special weekend? Make sure you have your partner's favorite team's jersey packed. No need to ask for amorous action, just put it on and approach him. His brain conditioning will kick in from there.

What's the cheap psychological trick? Sports have the potential to turn on your mate aggressively and sexually. Just show him the appropriate sports stimulus, and watch him transfer his passion for his team to you.

REFERENCES

Hillman, C., B.N. Cuthbert, J. Cauraugh, M.M. Bradley, H.T. Schupp, and P.J. Lang. "We're #1: Sports Fans and Sports Pictures." *Psychophysiology* 34 (1997): S43.

Hillman, C., B. Cuthbert, H. Schupp, and P. Lang. "Team Rivalry: Motivated Attention in Die-Hard Football Fans." *Psychophysiology* 35 (1998): S40.

Pavlov, I. *Conditioned Reflexes: An Investigation of the Physiological Activity of the Cerebral Cortex.* London: Oxford University Press, 1927.

Cheap Trick No. 37

Seduce Me,
Now and Forever

In the United States, 79 percent of male and 63 percent of female college-age students admit to premarital sexual relations. After they marry, it's not unusual for couples—even those who were the most sexually active—to experience a letdown. Take a look at the numbers. Sexual activity is frequent among newly married couples (average frequency is fifteen times a month). After a couple is married for fifteen years, this rate drops over 50 percent to an average of six times a month. Blame it on the routine of work and marriage; many couples fall into "the sexual rut." Same way. Same day. Same time. Same place. Too much of the same thing can lead to a dull marriage.

For a sexual relationship to thrive, the art of seduction and a playful attitude must be kept alive. On this point, researchers agree. To avoid the common trap of a dull and routine sex life, get creative and surprise your mate. Be aware that there is a broad dimension to sexuality—it's not just the act of intercourse. As your relationship expands, let your physical expression of love for each other grow and develop as well.

What's the cheap psychological trick? Variety is the spice of life.

REFERENCES

Michael, R., J.H. Gagnon, E.O. Laumann, and G. Kolata. *Sex in America: A Definitive Survey.* Boston: Little Brown, 1994.

 # PART IV

Affairing and Repairing

Navigating the Rocky Road of Romance

Love is an exploding cigar
which we willingly smoke.

—Lynda Barry

Cheap Trick No. 38

The Telltale Heart

Freud believed that somehow, some way, a person who is misbehaving will eventually do something to give him- or herself away. Freud also thought that because deep down these individuals want to be caught, their subconscious will finally allow the truth to pop out. Freudian slips are supposed to reveal a person's true thoughts and desires. Technically, these slipups are called "parapraxes." Modern detectives call them "tells" or "emblems." If you suspect a problem in your relationship, you can look for these telling behaviors, clues that your mate is not being faithful.

☀ Is your partner creating the "illusion of busy?" Is your lover all of a sudden working really long hours, not just the standard fifty- to sixty-hour week, but late-nighters and all-nighters? In addition to these exaggerated working hours, is there an increased number of evening wine-and-dines and out-of-town trips that don't include you? If so, your mate is either working incredibly hard or is trying to create in your mind the "illusion of busy."

❋ Do work sessions, evening entertainments, or trips seem to come up out of the blue? Most of the time, advanced warning is given for work requirements. Excuses for extra work activities that seem peculiar or strangely out-of-character are a red flag.

❋ Has your mate abruptly changed underwear style? Has he gone from boxers to bikinis without any coaxing from you? Has she put away her provocative teddies and started wearing only her dowdy pajamas or long-sleeved nightgowns? When men have affairs, they usually move to clothing they think make them look younger. When women stray, they choose to wear more conservative clothing around their mates.

❋ Has your mate suddenly started doing his own laundry? He may be washing his own clothes so you won't detect the "tells," such as lipstick marks or the scent of an unfamiliar perfume.

What's the cheap psychological trick? If you doubt your mate's fidelity, use these "tells" to help open your eyes. Keep in mind, however, that any one of these clues by itself does not point to misbehavior. Even several of the "tells" do not necessarily add up to proof of misconduct.

REFERENCES

Chebran, Y. *Bluff Your Way In Seduction*. London: Oval Books, 1999.

Greely, A.M. *Faithful Attractions*. New York: Tor Books, 1991.

Michael, R.T, J.H. Gagnon, E.O. Laumann, and G. Kolata. *Sex in America: A Definitive Survey*. Boston: Little, Brown, 1994.

Robinson, I., K. Ziss, B. Ganza, and Katz. "Twenty Years of the Sexual Revolution, 1965–1985: An Update." *Journal of Marriage & the Family* 53 (1991): 216–220.

Cheap Trick No. 39

Predicting the Future

A s lovers start to age, as relationships become routine, doubts and regrets—or suspicions that the other mate might be getting restless—may begin to surface. Some predictors can help you foresee the likelihood that an affair might disrupt your life together.

❋ *The Big Zero Birthdays.* Is your mate approaching 30, 40, 50, or even 60? These "transition" dates often precipitate regrets or feelings of inadequacy. At these natural demarcation points, you or your mate are more likely to question your relationship and perhaps begin to look around for greener pastures.

❋ A *friend's affair.* If a good friend says, "You know, I'm having an affair," adult peer pressure kicks in. At that point, the odds increase that one mate will succumb to another person's charms. When someone you know is having an affair, the act of infidelity may take on an everyday, common, no-big-deal flavor.

※ *The death of a parent.* When Mother or Father is no longer there to disapprove of misbehavior, it may free the son or daughter to get involved in an outside dalliance. An affair no longer threatens to bring on parental disapproval and the concomitant guilt.

※ *Fault-finding.* Do you often criticize your partner, or does your mate frequently pass judgment on you? If so, an affair may be in the making. Constant criticism can lower your mate's self-esteem and make him or her more likely to look for praise and respect from someone else.

What's the cheap psychological trick? Be aware of predictors that can indicate troubled times ahead in your relationship. Life may be "telling" you what you need to know.

REFERENCE

Michael R., J. Gagnon, E. Lauman, G. Kolata. *Sex in America: A Definitive Survey.* Boston: Little Brown, 1994.

Cheap Trick No. 40

The Naked Truth

We live in a youth-worshipping culture. The media dictates our ideals to us—rippling biceps and washboard abs for men and round, supple breasts and long, slender legs for women. No matter your age, you are made to feel that if you want that competitive edge, you've got to dress young, look young, and act younger than you really are.

To get a handle on what's youthful and hip, you check out the magazines. Then you graduate to more and more graphic depictions of bodies. All of a sudden you notice that you're more and more uncomfortable with your partner and you are less and less satisfied with your own body. What happened? You played a cheap psychological trick on yourself!

An occasional look at a fashion magazine or the swimwear issue of a sports magazine and admiring the youthful models is, in general, harmless; the perusal of pictures of beautiful people should not result in any deleterious mental consequences. Looking at perfectly formed and erotically posed physical specimens, however, does involve some risks. Most of you know that obsessing on those ideals can wreak havoc on your own self-esteem, but you may not be aware of some other serious negative side effects from observing too many idealized body images.

Researchers asked a group of people to describe their mates before and after viewing magazines like *Playboy*, *Penthouse*, *Playgirl*, or even slides of abstract erotic art. The individuals taking part in the experiment rated their mate's appearance much lower after looking at the magazine. The images in the magazines showed them—explicitly and sometimes graphically—just what they were missing. But it didn't stop there!

Further evaluation by the researchers found that not only did looking at the pictures in the magazine cause people to find their mates less attractive, but it also resulted in a lower assessment of their love for their mates.

What's the cheap psychological trick? Either limit your ogling of centerfolds or remind yourself frequently that the images you are looking at are only a fantasy. Keep in mind that viewing the idealized bodies pictured in today's media can cause you to unfairly devalue your mate.

REFERENCES

"Pinups and Letdowns." *Psychology Today* 16 (1983): 83.

"Say It Isn't So"

Once upon a time the only two givens were death and taxes. Soon we'll be able to add affairs and lawsuits to that list. Researchers say from 40 to 75 percent of all married men eventually commit adultery; 25 to 43 percent of married women have affairs. But married couples don't have a monopoly on this problem. Infidelity can destroy any relationship. Even worse, the mere suspicion of unfaithfulness can have devastating results.

Suppose you suspect your lover of being unfaithful to you. Before you confront him or her and demand the truth, you should be aware of a phenomenon called "The Othello Error." To understand, you need to brush up on your Shakespeare.

Once upon a time there was a powerful Moor who married the fair Desdemona. So in love was he that jealousy, "the green-eyed monster," reared its ugly head. Of course, the monster had an accomplice, Othello's "trusted friend" Iago. To make a wonderfully long story short, Desdemona is accused of being unfaithful. She is innocent, and she protests her innocence—but to no avail. Othello interprets her emotional outbursts as proof of her infidelity. Tragically, he is convinced that her emotional state proves her guilt. That's the "Othello Error."

Many an innocent person accused of infidelity finds that protestations of innocence are easily misinterpreted. When people feel that another person doesn't believe them or thinks they're lying, emotions kick in. When people fear they won't be believed, their actions often make them look as if they're lying, even when they're telling the truth. In response to the stress, the tone and pitch of the accused person's voice changes. The listener perceives that the accused—to borrow a phrase from another Shakespearean play—"doth protest too much" and mentally finds the accused guilty. Overemotional protests of innocence are frequently construed as a statement of guilt—even in divorce court. The harder the accused tries to prove his or her innocence, the more likely the Othello Error is to kick in.

What's the cheap psychological trick? If you suspect that your lover is being untrue to you, use caution when you force a confrontation. Remember that accusatory questions or out-and-out accusations will create tension and will probably produce an overwrought and defensive emotional response, making it almost impossible to get at the truth. Don't be trapped in the Othello Error. Work instead to create an atmosphere of trust so that the two of you can discuss your problems without accusations or defensiveness.

REFERENCE

"The Othello Error." Science Digest 1 (1988): 54–55.

Cheap Trick No. 42

Those
Lying Eyes

"Y̶ou can't hide those lying eyes." We are all familiar with the words to this popular Eagles hit. We
all depend on what we can see to substantiate
our beliefs. Some say that 90 percent of what we learn
comes through visual clues. But the truth is some people
can lie without detection because unfortunately most of us
tend to rely on the *wrong* visual cues to determine whether
or not a person is prevaricating. When you are concerned
that your partner is not being completely truthful with you,
make sure you know what to look for—some visual clues
are more reliable indicators of lying than others.

Reliable signs that a person is lying:

❋ Shrugs and blinks. When people are lying, they
shrug and blink a lot.

✸ Adaptive behaviors. When liars realize they are beginning to show their nervousness, they may use adaptive behaviors to stop this jitteriness. For instance, they may pour a drink, smoke a cigarette, or simply hold something to hide the trembling of their hands.

✸ Emblems. Every day we use body movements called emblems to express ourselves in normal conversation. Emblems are physical "stand-for" behaviors—like making the "okay" sign with the thumb and index finger. Under stress, emblems can be more like slips of the tongue (or body) and may reveal more than the person's words.

✸ Illustrators. People often emphasize or "illustrate" what they are saying with gestures like jabbing their finger in the air or pounding their fist on the table. Pay attention to what a person says, especially if the words are accompanied by an "illustrator." They are likely to be telling the truth. As a general rule, because liars do not want their words to be inspected that closely, they do not call attention to them with strong gestures.

✸ Perspiration. When people fear being caught in a lie, emotions and involuntary reactions like sweating may be heightened. Remember the scene in the movie *Total Recall* when the hero believes a scientist's words until he notices a "telling behavior?" One distinct bead of sweat emerging from a perfectly composed face gives the lying scientist away, and he is dispatched quickly to another dimension.

Unreliable signs that a person is lying:

☀ A smile. Don't be so quick to interpret a smile as a sign of insincerity. People who are lying smile less than truth tellers.

☀ Direct eye contact. Habitual liars know that people distrust others who "can't look me in the eye" so they are likely to go out of their way to make eye contact.

☀ Fidgeting. This behavior is often misinterpreted. Liars know that people look for this visual clue, and they may make a concerted effort to sit still instead.

☀ Manipulators. These behaviors—such as squirming, scratching, pushing back one's hair, rubbing or picking at one's body—may indicate nervousness, but they are not proof of lying.

☀ Duping delight. Polygraph examiners know that some liars are quite good at deceiving and take great delight in getting away with deception. Many liars love the thrill of the chase, and as a result, they chase the thrill. They may even manifest a screwy kind of glee when you're questioning them.

What's the cheap psychological trick? If you suspect your partner is being less than truthful with you, don't depend on conventional wisdom to help you determine if they are lying and don't always trust your eyes. Learn to recognize the reliable signs that give liars away, and be aware that they are trying to fool you with an arsenal of cheap psychological tricks of their own.

REFERENCES

Ekman, P. *Telling Lies: Clues to Deceit in the Marketplace, Politics, and Marriage.* New York: Norton, 1985.

Holtgroves, T., and A.R. Grayer. "I am not a Crook: Effects of Denials on Perceptions of a Defendant's Guilt, Personality, and Motives." *Journal of Applied Social Psychology* 24 (1994): 2132–2150.

Cheap Trick No. 43

Sick Words

At times, especially in the heat of anger, we all say things to the ones we love that are meant to hurt. Be careful or you may say something to your lover that you will regret for a lifetime. Even if you apologize and gain forgiveness, your negative words may ring in your partner's head for a long time—partly because the human brain tends to remember negative events longer than positive ones, but mostly because people fear being hurt again.

Certain kinds of comments—even tongue-in-cheek, teasing remarks—can be destructive to a relationship, especially if they are repeated frequently. We all know that words have the potential to inflict dangerous psychological wounds. But the damage may go deeper. Disparaging words can actually make your mate physically ill. Some psychologists call these hurtful phrases "words that wound."

Communication can be the key to keeping a relationship healthy, but the wrong kind of communication weakens it and can even make one *or both* partners sick. When researchers studied how females use their verbal skills within a relationship, they found that the women in stable, peaceful relationships used words in ways that caused their mates to love them more. In rocky relationships, the females tended to use their verbal skills to inflict pain on their partners. Even when the partners managed to arrange a truce, the pain did not go away. This kind of hurtful communication increased stress levels and kept hormone levels high. Over time the strain on the hormone system increased the possibility of everyday illnesses like the common cold and in some cases may have contributed to the development of more serious diseases like cancer and heart disease. While that study focused mainly on females, other researchers have found that men are equally capable of harming their partners with "words that wound."

What's the cheap psychological trick? Every couple has disagreements, and almost every couple fights about something from time to time. When you argue, avoid words that wound. Stick to the facts related to the problem at hand, and don't bring up pet peeves that have nothing to do with the current discussion. At times of stress, stay away from comments on your mate's appearance or sexual performance, and steer clear of comparisons. If anger seems to be getting out of control, walk away, buy a little time, and continue the discussion later.

Words are powerful tools. Used correctly, they can strengthen or heal a relationship. Used incorrectly, they can cause pain and sickness even long after victims of hurtful words have forgiven their thoughtless partners.

REFERENCES

Druckman, A. "Words that Wound." *Psychology Today* 32 September-October (1999): 13.
Mason, A. *The Bluffer's Guide to Men*. London: Ravette Publishing, 1998.
Muratore, M. *The Bluffer's Guide to Women*. London: Oval Books, 1999.
Nisbett, R.E. *Rules for Reasoning*. Hillsdale, NJ: Erlbaum Associates, 1993.

The Merry-Go-Round from Hell

People are unfaithful to their lovers for many reasons. The obvious one is that they're sexually frustrated either physically or psychologically. But believe it or not, affairs are often not about sex. The reasons men and women have affairs are as diverse as the people having them, but among the more common reasons are the inability to communicate with each other, the feeling of being underappreciated, the need for more companionship, or the desire for adventure.

No matter what's motivating the affair, it's amazing how quickly the persons involved realize how expensive it is, how much guilt and shame it creates, how far from perfect the new lover is, and how nice it would be just to get out.

Yet, for some reason, affairs seem to take on a life of their own and keep going long after they should have ended. People having an affair can find themselves trapped in a vicious circle—caught in a psychological rut, unable to break free.

Think of an affair as the "merry-go-round from hell." Ups and downs, round and round, no exit, physiological pleasure or release at every turn, and, of course, the tarnished brass ring. What keeps a person on that cursed merry-go-round, riding bareback with someone else? The force that holds the illicit lovers locked on course can sometimes be explained by the "drive reduction theory." It works like this.

Once upon a time, the "eyes meet from across the room" and the cycle starts. As soon as the pair steps on the merry-go-round and takes that initial spin—the first sexual encounter—a myriad of emotions sets in. Typically, affairs cause both pleasure and anxiety. The anxiety grows and grows, gnaws and gnaws, and adds to the pressures in everyday life. To reduce this anxiety, the errant mate decides to see the new lover one more time and jumps on that carousel again. While riding the merry-go-round, pleasures override the anxiety, and "all's right with the world." The immediate feel-good emotions from the affair overshadow the problems at home or at work. And the merry-go-round goes round and round and round and round…

The anxiety and discomfort of people involved in affairs diminish when they are with the person they think they love. The fact that the anxiety—felt so strongly at home or in the presence of the betrayed partner—can be reduced to almost nothing in the company of the new lover indirectly tricks the brain into thinking that the "affair is the right thing to do."

Typically, it is negatively charged events—sexually transmitted diseases, work transfers to another city, blackmail, illness—that disrupt the affair and return the wayward partner to the fold. Unfortunately, these situations are fraught with anxiety that can just as easily push him or her right back into the affair.

What's the cheap psychological trick? Beware the drive reduction cycle. Don't get on that merry-go-round from hell in the first place.

REFERENCE

Hull, C.L. *Principles of Behavior.* New York: Appleton-Century-Crofts, 1942.
Hull, C.L. *Essentials of Behavior.* New Haven, Connecticut: Yale University Press, 1951.

Six Months Support

So you've called it quits. You've thought it through, and you've both decided that breaking up is the only logical course of action. Whether the separation was amicable or hostile, the relationship is over and you are ready to get on with your life. Anything should be easy after the struggle you've been through, right? Not necessarily. Many people say, in retrospect, that the pain of breaking up was the easy part compared to the sinking feelings ("I'm all alone now." "How will I manage?" "The house feels like a tomb.") that take over when the separation is final. After a breakup, you may feel overwhelmed with all the responsibilities you must now face alone. Your finances may be in disarray, you may have children to raise or educate, or you may feel completely incompetent to care for a house by yourself.

Most counselors will tell you that if you can get through the first six months after a breakup or a divorce, you can get through a lifetime. Some people fall apart and take years to recover after a breakup. Some of them have to spend a great deal of time and money working their problems out with the help of professionals. (If you are one of these people, make sure the counselor or therapist you seek out has legitimate credentials, received accredited training, and is properly licensed. A lot of charlatans are ready and willing to take money from vulnerable people looking for easy answers to their problems.)

Others seem to sail through this difficult time. What did these people do that the others did not? They had a team of experts at their beck and call, waiting in the wings to answer any question and resolve any crisis. And they didn't have to pay a therapist with an advanced degree or bare their souls for hours in front of a group of twelve strangers.

Researchers have found that people who reached out to others for advice and took action adjusted more quickly, felt better about themselves, made more new friends, and had fewer financial problems than people who chose to analyze their pain and dwell on their losses.

What's the cheap psychological trick? After a long-term relationship dissolves and you are left alone feeling helpless, create your own support group. If you're lucky, you'll only need it for six months or so. Find yourself a series of experts—grandparents, professionals, ministers, rabbis, priests, work-at-home moms and dads, even Internet penpals—who are willing to help you answer any question you have, no matter how short the notice. The support group you build yourself will be action oriented. You won't be wasting your time wringing your hands and rehashing your woes. Put a semblance of control back in your life—you'll recover faster.

REFERENCE

Price, R.H., E.L. Cowen, R.P. Lorian, and J. Ramos-McKay (Eds.) *Fourteen Ounces of Prevention: A Casebook for Practitioners.* Washington, D.C.: American Psychological Association, 1988.

Can We Still Be Friends?

What's the opposite of love? An off-the-cuff answer is usually "hate." But hate is not the opposite of love. The opposite of love—and hate—is indifference.

After a breakup, you may find it hard to adjust. Your relationship may be finished physically, but inside your head, it may not be over for years. You may still love your ex-partner or hate your ex-wife. The two of you may still be friendly or you may feel hostile toward each other. Or you both may be so glad to be out of the relationship you don't think about each other at all! Which route is the way toward repairing and healing? Researchers looked into this question and came up with some surprising results.

If the hostility still rages when your ex-partner's name is mentioned, you're not adjusting as well as you could. Your hate may be holding you back and keeping you from moving on.

If you still feel preoccupied with the pain of the recent breakup, you may be stuck in the past when you should be thinking about your future.

Even if you are on friendly terms with your ex-lover, you could still be stuck! You may be dependent in some ways on your ex or you may be harboring unrealistic fantasies about reconciliation. After a breakup, when your former partner asks, "Can we still be friends?" maybe your answer should be, "Let's wait and see."

So what is the quickest way to recover when a relationship falls apart?

The researchers concluded that after a breakup, the people who did not nurture a feeling of hostility, who weren't preoccupied with the events of the breakup, and who really didn't give a tinker's damn found it easier to get over the pain and get on with their lives.

What's the cheap psychological trick? After a breakup, remember that the opposite of love is not hate. It is indifference. Get some distance from your hurt and disappointment by repeating these magic phrases to yourself:

"I don't care about that now,"

"It's over now, and that's all there is to it," and

"I'm over it now and I'm ready to think about other things."

Once you can say any one of these phrases and truly mean it, you'll be well on your way to recovery.

REFERENCE

Paul, A.M. "Importance of Indifference." *Psychology Today* 30 September–October (1997): 20.

Cheap Trick No. 47

Sit Right Down and Write Yourself a Letter

It can take many months to recover from the hurt and pain generated by a breakup. During that time, you need to talk about your feelings, and you naturally turn to your friends. After several weeks of talking to the same people about the same subject, however, you may begin to notice that when you start in on your travails your friends smile politely and try to change the flow of the conversation—or simply look for a way to get out of the conversation altogether.

If you have been betrayed or jilted, or if you have just gone through a divorce, chances are you do indeed have a lot to complain about. After a divorce, a female's standard of living takes, on the average, a 27 percent nosedive. A newly divorced male may experience a slight rise in standard of living, but he is likely to be far unhappier than his ex—partly because men perceive that the system works against them and that people may judge them more harshly. Because men believe they have less control over things like custody and child support, their resentment tends to grow.

Psychological research is clear on this point: Whether you're male or female, the fact remains that after a painful breakup, it will do you good to talk about it. You do not, however, always have to talk about it with someone else. Try talking to yourself!

First, quit trying *not* to think about all the problems that have been thrown your way. By some strange quirk of brain wiring, the more you try *not* to think about something, the more your brain dwells on it. Go ahead and think about your pain and suffering; that sometimes gets those thoughts out of your brain's active file and clears up some mental breathing room.

Next, talk it out—on paper! Take the excellent advice expressed in the old song: "I'm going to sit right down and write myself a letter." Writing by hand works best. There's something about thinking about a problem methodically, then working it out of the brain, down through the hand and fingers, and finally onto the paper, that is healing to the brain. The act of writing yourself a series of letters explaining everything you've been through— how angry you are, how much you resent your former partner, how much time and money you've wasted—is quite healing and adds up to cheap therapy.

In your first letter, introduce the problem to an imaginary friend. Start the letter with, "You won't believe what's happened to me over the last year...."

In your next epistle, get graphic! This letter is for your eyes only, so you can get just as vulgar, and "sex-plicit" as you like. It doesn't matter whether you feel that you're the innocent or the offending party; either way you have hurts that need to be aired.

In your next letter focus on the pain other members of your family are going through. It's important to write this one because it will help you recognize that you're not as alone in this as you thought you were.

And finally, write a letter that describes what you're doing to resolve this problem, to get a handle on it, and to move on with your life.

When you're hurting, it's healthy to talk about the mental and physical pain you're going through. If you have at least one good friend who listens, you're more than lucky—you're blessed. But there are times when even the best of friends deserves a break from your worries.

What's the cheap psychological trick? Sit right down and write yourself a series of letters. Detail your hopes, fears, worries, pains, dreams, and most important of all, your plans to get yourself out of this mess with your health in tact. It works. And when you feel better, burn the letters.

REFERENCES

Jackson, D. "Men are Less Happy Postdivorce: The Healing Power of Confiding in Others." *New Woman* 27 (1997): 49.

Pennebaker, J.W. *Opening Up*. New York: William Morrow, 1990.

Pennebaker, J.W., M. Colder, and L.K. Sharp. "Accelerating the Coping Process." *Journal of Personality and Social Psychology* 58 (1990): 528–537.

 # PART V

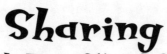 ## Sharing
Spending the Rest of Your Life Together

Love is like playing the piano. Not until
you learn to play by the rules can you forget
the rules and play by heart.

—*Anonymous*

Cheap Trick No. 48

The Blame Game

It's easier to assign blame than it is to accept it. Young children learn early to deny guilt. Subsequently, when the parent asks "Did you break that?" the first word out of the child's mouth is "no." When the teacher inquires about missing homework, the student responds with a stock excuse. As people get older, they invent ever more sophisticated ways to avoid responsibility when things go wrong. This habit can get you in trouble when you are trying to build a lasting relationship.

Marriage counselors know their work is cut out for them when one or both partners respond to problems with phrases like "It's not my fault," "It's your problem, now you fix it," "I don't want to hear about it," and "You'll never change." These expressions reveal an unwillingness to take a share of the blame for the problem, to accept any responsibility for it, or to help find a solution for it.

On the other hand, counselors are encouraged when they hear their clients say "I know I could do better," "I'm at fault too," "I'm so sorry—how can I make it up to you," and "Here's what I think we need to do." The old Danish proverb says it best: "Faults are thick where love is thin." The experts know that the degree of love in a relationship is positively correlated to the willingness of the partners to share the blame and to work together to fix problems.

What's the cheap psychological trick? When difficulties arise between you and your lover, use the fifty-fifty rule. Ask yourselves, "How much of this problem is my responsibility?" Then meet each other halfway, take your fair share of the blame, and join forces to resolve the problem.

REFERENCE

Edwards, R. "New tools help gauge marital success." *APA Monitor* February (1998): 6.

Kurdek, L.A. "Predicting Marital Dissolution: A 5-year Prospective Longitudinal Study of Newlywed Couples." *Journal of Personality and Social Psychology* 64 (1993) 221–242.

Van Lange, P.A.M. & C.E. Rusbult. "My Relationship is Better Than—and Not as Bad as—Yours Is! The Perception of Superiority in Close Relationships." *Personality and Social Psychology Bulletin* 21 (1995) 32–44.

The Great
Escape

From time to time, every relationship faces difficulties. When one partner feels uncomfortable, anxious, or pressured about the relationship, that person will look for something, *anything*, to relieve the anxiety. Some people turn to a physical affair; others seek a different form of escape—work, school, church, a new hobby, sports, even alcohol. In fact, any activity that will take their mind off their home problems and reduce their worries about the relationship can qualify as a "great escape."

Engaging in any of these activities is not necessarily detrimental to a partnership. However, when one partner habitually uses other pursuits to "buy time" or to "escape" the pressures of the relationship, the two lovers begin to drift apart and the bond between them will inevitably be weakened. The good news is that in these kinds of escape, no "other man" or "other woman" is involved. The bad news is that there is no one to confront or blame. When a relationship is threatened by competition from outside activities, it usually takes longer to figure out what's going on, and it is harder to acknowledge that the relationship is drifting apart.

At the first sign that your partner is distancing him- or herself from you, find a "superordinate goal" and implement it quickly. A superordinate goal is one that takes precedence over other less important goals. It is "super" because both members of the partnership are interested in doing, learning, or experiencing it.

Try to find superordinate goals with minimal pressure.

Do both of you like to travel? If so, that's a superordinate goal. At the first sign of distancing, make sure the travel brochures are all over the house. This is the perfect time for the two of you to plan that special trip, whether it involves camping in the mountains or flying to India to see the "Taj Mahal"—truly a symbol of undying love.

Do both of you like working with your hands? Get involved and built a house for Habitat for Humanity.

Do both of you like antiques? Take a road trip and explore flea markets together.

Do both of you like gardening? Plan a new garden area in the backyard or on the patio and plant it together.

What's the cheap psychological trick? When you feel your lover drifting away from you, substitute an escape for one with a mutually pleasurable escape for two. A new activity that you both can enjoy will open up communication channels and help you find ways to make the relationship work better. Using a superordinate goal accentuates commonalities and helps you reestablish shared interests, which is why you got together in the first place.

REFERENCE

Laumann, E.O., J.H. Gagnon, R.T. Michael, and S. Michaels. *The Social Organization of Sexuality: Sexual Practices in the United States.* Chicago: University of Chicago Press, 1994.

The Shortest, Cheapest, and Most Difficult Trick in the Book

Next to "I love you," what are the three most beautiful words in the English language? "I'm so sorry." Okay, so it's four words if you expand the contraction. You could get away with the three words "I am sorry," but the adverb "so" will intensify the expression and get your feelings across more effectively.

Remember, though, that merely repeating these contrite words may not return you to your partner's good graces unless your actions show that you are sincere.

What's the cheap psychological trick? Repeat the phrase "I'm so sorry" often, and then show that you mean it. Your behavior speaks much louder than words.

REFERENCE

Common sense and Grandma Buff

Flashbulb Memories

The story goes that the little girl paused just as she was preparing to blow out the candles on her birthday cake. Several seconds passed, and her mother asked, "What's taking you so long?" The wise child looked at her mother and said, "I'm making a memory."

This little girl had the right idea. We all develop memories in our mental darkrooms, but we don't always do it so that the memories will last. What makes certain memories stay with us so vividly while others fade away?

You are probably familiar with the term "flashbulb memory." This kind of recollection is a magical point in time when the world seems to stop for an instant, leaving you with an indelible image of an event etched in your brain. In a "flash," with no conscious effort on your part, the image is transformed into an "engram" that is almost impervious to decay. People can instantly recall where they were and what they were doing when they heard of President Kennedy's assassination, of the Challenger explosion, of Princess Diana's death. As "Old Rose" began to describe the fateful event of April 15, 1912, in the movie *Titanic*, she called up a flashbulb memory, saying, "I can still smell the fresh paint." Flashbulb memories preserve the sights, the sounds, the smells, and the emotions of out-of-the-ordinary experiences.

Wouldn't you like to remember the special events of your life with your partner with the same intensity of a flashbulb memory? You can if you will involve your senses. During special occasions, notice smells, colors, and sounds. Touch something and make a mental note of how it feels. The more senses you involve in this process, the more likely you are to "engram" the images in your brain. Make it a point to replay the event often over the next few days, talk about it with your partner, and review it in the weeks to follow. If possible, keep a tangible souvenir of the moment—a pressed flower in a book, a ticket to a concert, a bit of wrapping paper.

A similar method of memory enhancement can even ease the trauma of sad or tragic events. Until time can heal your pain, use a technique called "reciprocal inhibition" to weaken the sad memory. On the anniversary of a sad event, focus on something happy, on something pleasant that happens during that day. Make a mental recording of the smells, sounds, tastes, and excitement of this more lighthearted event, and on the next anniversary of the sad event, you will have a good memory to mitigate the pain.

What's the cheap psychological trick? Enhance the relationship with your lover by making memories that last. Bring all your senses into play and preserve the special moments for a lifetime. And remember, flashbulb memories endure even longer when they are shared with someone you love.

REFERENCES

Brown, R., and J. Kulik. "Flashbulb Memories." *Cognition* 5 (1997) 73–99.

To Forgive
Is Divine

Forgiving is easier to talk about than it is to do. It's easy to say, "I forgive you," but to do it right, it takes more than these three little words—and it is important to your health and to the endurance of your relationship for you to do it right.

When your lover has said the magic words, "I'm so sorry," and you have reciprocated with the phrase, "I forgive you," everything may return to normal and the two of you can get back to building a stronger relationship. Sometimes, however, when you tell your partner "I forgive you," your subconscious keeps telling you "something's not quite right." You feel anxious and unhappy, and your physical state even begins to show the strain.

Maybe your "forgiveness" is doing more harm than good because you have granted it for one of these wrong (and wrongheaded) reasons.

☼ Saying you forgive someone just to avoid additional conflict or because you feel trapped.

☼ Offering forgiveness only because it is expected of you or because you think it is the polite thing to do.

☼ Granting your pardon to show that you are a better, more mature, or more sensitive person than your offending partner.

☼ Declaring that you forgive your partner while plotting revenge. (Remember that revenge doesn't have to be an overt act. It can be accomplished quite effectively through passive-aggressive behavior or through behind-the-back maneuverings.)

Withholding sincere forgiveness for one of the first three reasons does nothing to resolve problems between you and your partner and can even damage the relationship between you, but offering a false forgiveness while maintaining resentment and anger can be downright hazardous to your health.

Research shows that refusing to forgive, harboring a desire for revenge, or nursing a hatred for the offending party is harmful to the heart. The exact mechanism by which this manifests is not clearly understood. It is generally thought that withholding forgiveness, continually dwelling on past grievances, and maintaining hostility keeps you in a constant state of overvigilance and keeps your stress level high.

What's the cheap psychological trick? To err is human; to forgive, divine. Learn to be forgiving. It is not only an essential skill in developing a relationship, but it is also good for your physical and mental well-being. Forgive for the right reasons and reap the benefits. And if you can't figure out how to forgive on your own, get some professional assistance from a licensed expert. Your heart—and your partner—will thank you for it.

REFERENCES

Layton, M. "Can you Forgive Him?" *Child* October (1997): 67.

Marshall, G.N., C.B. Wortman, R.R. Vickers, J.W. Kusulas, and L.K. Hewig. "The Five-Factor Model of Personality As a Framework for Personality-Related Research." *Journal of Personality & Social Psychology* 67 (1994): 278–286.

Cheap Trick No. 53

Social Ties

When males are young, they tend to have many friends, and females tend to have a select few. However, as people age, this trend reverses. As males age, they have fewer male friends, but as females grow older, they have more female friends. Could that be one reason that women live longer than men?

Research is now suggesting that the more friends you have, the more social ties you have to the community, the healthier you tend to stay. As odd as it may seem, studies have clearly shown that social ties and illness are *negatively* correlated: the more friends you have, the less likely you are to get a cold. Apparently, social ties can be more effective than Mom's chicken soup. But more importantly, having a wide circle of friends gives you a reason to live and enhances what many healers call your "somatic compliance."

Somatic compliance is your body's tendency to do what you wish it to do. In other words, if you have someone to

live for, someone to stay healthy for, your brain passes this thought on to your body, and your immunity system is strengthened. That's one reason a happy marriage can help you live longer. But if you want to increase your odds for enjoying your golden years, reach out and create more ties to other people and to your community.

What's the cheap psychological trick? Women already seem to have mastered this trick. Men, now it is your turn. The solid relationship with your partner is a good start, but you need to start establishing more social ties. They are good for you. Take that old saying to heart: "Make new friends and keep the old. One is silver and the other gold."

REFERENCES

Jones, D.C. and K. Vaughan. "Close Friendships Among Senior Adults." *Psychology and Aging* 5 (1990): 451–457.

Rivera, P.A., J.M. Rose, A. Futterman, S.B. Lovett, and D. Galagher-Thompson. "Dimensions of Perceived Social Support in Clinically Depressed and Non-Depressed Female Caregivers." *Psychology and Aging* 6 (1991): 232–237.

Uchino, B.N., J.T. Cacioppo, and J.K. Kiecolt-Glaser. "The Relationship Between Social Support and Physiological Processes." *Psychological Bulletin* 119 (1996): 488–531.

Cheap Trick No. 54

Oh, My God!

In the past decade, researchers conducted a number of studies on churchgoing and other religious practices. One study found that regular churchgoers tended to be fatter than people who did not attend church. Another came up with evidence for a religious "gene" that might explain why some twins separated at birth display an identical level of religious intensity when they reach adulthood. But other findings had more serious implications for healthy relationships.

Studies show that religious faith can facilitate mental and physical health. Research conducted in the 1950s demonstrated that prayer often plays a therapeutic role in disease reduction. Numerous double-blind studies show that prayer can expedite healing and ease the pain of asthma, anxiety, and heart disease, as well as high and low blood pressure. Results from a recent study suggest that religious faith can hasten recovery from mild to moderate depression. Other researchers believe that the absence of spirituality correlates with higher rates of illness.

The implication seems to be that religious faith can help keep you and your mate healthy and happy, and that cannot hurt a relationship. Religion has held people together for ages. It might also strengthen the bonds of unity between you and your partner.

At its best, religion supports families in their trials and in their celebrations. It is an anchor that can keep love steady and a discipline that nurtures mutual care, respect, and loyalty.

What's the cheap psychological trick? Well, let's get serious here. Religious faith cannot be a cheap psychological trick. It is demanding, and it can require sacrifice and service to other people. But it can also deepen and enrich your life and the lives of those you love. It can heighten the "for better" and palliate the "for worse." It can minimize the pain of sickness and increase the pleasures of health.

You can never know where religious faith might lead you. But daring to live a life filled with surprises may be the best psychological trick of all.

REFERENCES

Bower, B. "Listening to Faith as a Balm for Depression." *Science News* 153 (1998): 247.

Waller, N.G., B.A. Kojetin, T.J. Bouchard, D.T. Lykken, and A. Tellegen. "Genetic and Environmental Influences on Religious Interests, Attitudes, and Values: A Study of Twins Reared Apart and Together." *Psychological Science* 1 (1990): 138–142.

Waller, N.G., and P.R. Shaver. "The Importance of Nongenetic Influences on Romantic Love Styles: A Twin-Family Study." *Psychological Science* 5 (1994): 268–274.

Cheap Trick No. 55

A Happy Ending

All good things must come to an end. Even the longest life, as the end nears, seems short. Not all couples have the opportunity to celebrate their silver, golden, or diamond anniversaries together. Whether the end of a relationship is due to divorce or death, the remaining partner has to deal with a profound sense of loss and the inevitable pain associated with it.

Freud explained that we grieve because our love for—and our need for love from—absent partners does not stop when they are gone. We cannot turn our love—or our need for love— off like a light switch. We are accustomed to giving love and having our love reciprocated. When we lose a partner, we grieve not only over the loss of that person who has been so important to us, but we also grieve over our loss of love.

Grief is a natural human process, and the ways of coping with grief are numerous and varied. Our personalities and cultural conventions determine how we manage during our times of mourning. Yet, some people seem to be able to deal with their loss and the inevitable pain associated with it and get on with their lives more quickly and more easily than others are. They seem to have discovered a healthier and more mature way of grieving.

Instead of obsessing on the pain and loneliness they feel at losing their loved one, these fortunate people know to focus on what a privilege it was to know and to grow with that person. Rather than concentrating on questions like "What am I going to do without him?" "How can I live without her?" or "Where am I going to go from here?" they use phrases like "It was pleasure to know him," "It was a privilege to call her a friend," "I was lucky to know her," and "It was a joy to be married to him."

What's the cheap psychological trick? There is nothing cheap and nothing tricky about this approach to grief. Focus on the privilege of a life shared, review the things the two of you learned and enjoyed together, and relive the good—and bad—times associated with your relationship. An objective examination of the special moments you shared together will help you get past your sorrow and help you look forward to building new relationships with others.

REFERENCES

Rakowski, W. Cited in Margoshes, P. "For Many, Old Age is the Prime of Life." *APA Monitor* 26 (5) (1995): 36–37.

Stroebe, M.S., M.M. Gergen, K.J. Gergen, and W. Stroebe. "Broken Hearts or Broken Bonds: Love and Death in Historical Perspective." *American Psychologist* 47 (1992): 1205–1212.

ABOUT THE AUTHOR

Perry Buffington is a psychologist, author, lecturer, and media personality. His "Cheap Psychological Tricks" column is syndicated to newspapers and online services through Universal Press Syndicate. Buffington's seminars on creativity, leadership, and charisma have received international acclaim. He is the author of hundreds of articles and numerous books, including CHEAP PSYCHOLOGICAL TRICKS; ARCHIVAL ATLANTA; RIGHT TIME, RIGHT PLACE, RIGHT MOVE, RIGHT NOW; and YOUR BEHAVIOR IS SHOWING. Dr. Buffington lives in Florida.

ABOUT THE ILLUSTRATOR

Jen Singh grew up in St. Joseph, Michigan, and studied illustration at Kendall College of Art & Design in Grand Rapids. After graduation, she moved to Atlanta, where she has worked as an artist ever since. She now lives in Decatur, Georgia, with husband J.T. and her two cats.